PROTECTING
THE
PRESIDENT

☆

PROTECTING
THE
PRESIDENT

The Inside Story
of a Secret Service Agent

by DENNIS V. N. McCARTHY
with PHILIP W. SMITH

WILLIAM MORROW AND COMPANY, INC.

NEW YORK

Library of Congress Cataloging in Publication Data

McCarthy, Dennis V. N.
  Protecting the president.

  Includes index.
  1. McCarthy, Dennis V. N. 2. United States.
Secret Service—Officials and employees—Biography.
3. Presidents—United States—Protection. I. Smith,
Philip W. (Philip Wayne), 1945–   . II. Title.
HV7911.M387A37 1985   363.2'8 [B]   85-13737
ISBN 0-688-05422-6

Printed in the United States of America

First Edition

1 2 3 4 5 6 7 8 9 10

BOOK DESIGN BY BOB FREESE

To Shelby
for two fine sons
and the good years we shared

Preface

This book is an attempt to portray, as honestly and straightforwardly as possible, what it is like to be a special agent in the United States Secret Service.

Few other jobs in the world demand more of the people who do them. Secret Service agents must deal with everything from the criminal world of counterfeiting run by small-time hoodlums, to big-time organized crime, to the world's heads of state. Agents' jobs take them to places few people ever see and put them in daily contact with some of the world's most powerful men and women. But for all the glamour and excitement, there are countless hours of standing alone in deserted hotel corridors outside a door behind which the President is sleeping. And there is the constant stress of never knowing which face in the crowd might be another Lee Harvey Oswald or Arthur Bremer or Sara Jane Moore.

Few other jobs in the world require the combination of nerve, judgment, and instant reflexes demanded daily of a Secret Service

agent on a protective detail. But Secret Service agents aren't su-
permen and -women. They get angry. They feel pity. They even
cry sometimes.

This is the story of one Secret Service agent and some of the
men and women he worked with and for between 1964 and 1984.
It's not the all-encompassing story of the Secret Service. Its perspective is not that of headquarters, but that of the agent on the
street, the shift leader on the midnight watch at the White
House, the guy the President calls when the White House starts
closing in and he wants to go for a ride, or whom the First Lady
calls when she wants to go to the beauty parlor.

This is not an exposé. Great care has been taken to avoid revealing any information that might be useful to a potential assassin. Anyone looking for the number of agents on a security detail,
what kind of weapons they carry, their code words and procedures won't find the answers here. What readers will find is that
Secret Service agents are human beings, trying to do a job that's
often damn near impossible.

Many people helped make this book possible. Some of them want
no public recognition, but they know who they are and that they
have our thanks. To many friends at The Class Reunion, one of
Washington's favorite press and political gathering places
through four presidential administrations, our thanks for much
good advice on how to put this story together.

We owe a special debt of gratitude to three veteran Washington correspondents—Joe Volz of the New York *Daily News*,
Rudy Abramson of the *Los Angeles Times*, and Mick Rood of
the *Harrisburg Patriot-News*—for reading some of the early drafts
and contributing their valuable insight. Special thanks also to
Sunday Fellows of the *New York Times* Washington bureau for
her research help, and to Sara Jennett for her assistance with
typing.

And most of all, our thanks to Susan Smith for countless hours of help with research, indexing, editing, and typing and for putting up with us during the more than three years that this project was under way.

Dennis V. N. McCarthy
Philip W. Smith

Contents

PROTECTING
THE
PRESIDENT

Prologue

The spectators lining the sidewalk across T Street reacted as soon as the President walked through the door of the hotel. I have watched this scene thousands of times at hundreds of locations all over the world. It is always the same. Even from a distance, you can read the words "There he is" on the lips of several people. Then, following an instant of silence, come the cheers and shouts of "Mr. President! Over here, Mr. President!"

My back was turned to the hotel's VIP entrance as I scanned the area for signs of trouble. There were none.

Everything about the day until this moment had been routine. There were no demonstrators. Just a group of some two hundred ordinary citizens waiting to catch a glimpse of the President. It would take him just a few seconds to walk the twenty-five feet from the hotel door to the armored limousine that sat in the driveway with its engine running, waiting to take him back to the White House.

Then suddenly, to my left, I heard a pop no louder than a firecracker going off. Almost instantly the sound came again and I realized that it wasn't a firecracker.

Someone was firing a weapon!

I whirled to the left, but could see nothing except a line of television cameramen with portable cameras on their shoulders, filming the President as he walked toward the car, waving to the crowd and surrounded by Secret Service agents and members of his staff.

Here it was. The moment I had waited for, thought about, constantly trained for, and dreaded throughout the sixteen and a half years that I had been a United States Secret Service special agent.

I remember a feeling of panic. Not fear, but panic, because I could hear shots but I couldn't see where they were coming from or who was doing the shooting.

I had to get to that gun.

The natural human instinct in such a situation is to move away from danger. Even the best-trained combat troops and police SWAT teams are taught to dive for cover the moment they come under fire.

I have never thought of myself as a hero, and I don't today, but years of training and a desire to do the job I was being paid to do made me react as I did.

By the third shot, I saw two hands gripping a pistol between the television cameras.

The gun was about eight feet away and I dived for it.

As I flew through the air, I saw a man in a crouched firing position pulling the trigger as fast as he could. I'm not sure if he was moving forward as he fired or if those around him were moving backward, making him appear to be advancing.

I recall the scene vividly, but only in shades of gray, like a black-and-white movie.

I came down in the middle of the gunman's back just as he fired the last bullet in the pistol. I wrapped my right arm around his head and reached for the gun with my left hand. As I landed on him, he collapsed under my weight. It was as if at that moment he gave up completely, surrendering to whatever fate awaited him.

But as we went down, I could hear the rapid click, click, click of the hammer hitting an empty chamber as he continued to squeeze the trigger after firing the six shots the pistol held.

He said nothing and offered no resistance.

As I reached for the gun, he dropped it to the pavement and I never saw it again.

Though in the next few days I would go through a brief period of blaming myself for not having acted quickly enough, in less than two seconds I had earned my salary for twenty years as a Secret Service agent.

The date was March 30, 1981.

President Ronald Reagan had just finished giving a half-hour speech to four thousand members of the Building and Construction Trades Union at the Washington Hilton Hotel.

Several people at the hotel's T Street entrance, including myself, will never forget that gray spring afternoon.

A mentally disturbed twenty-five-year-old drifter named John W. Hinckley, Jr.—the product of a wealthy Colorado family— had changed our lives forever by shooting the President of the United States in a vain attempt to impress a young movie actress who, on that day, was three hundred miles north of Washington attending Yale University.

Apparently Hinckley had nothing against Ronald Reagan, either personally or politically. If he had any strong political views, he never revealed them. Hinckley was shooting at a symbol as much as, if not more than, he was shooting at a man.

Through a combination of good luck and the quick actions of a lot of highly trained security and medical people, Hinckley's attempt on the President's life did not succeed.

But if history is a guide, someday, somewhere, someone else will try again to kill a U.S. President.

When it happens, that person had better be prepared to take

on some of the world's best-trained and most dedicated law-enforcement officers. The Secret Service isn't perfect, but if there is a more professional group of thirty-five hundred men and women in the world, I am not aware of it.

I retired after twenty years in the Secret Service at the end of 1984, three years and nine months after President Reagan was shot. But the work of the service literally never stops. Every minute of every day, agents are on duty protecting the President, both as an individual and as a symbol of the government that he leads.

CHAPTER 1

White House Detail

When the President finished speaking, he stood up behind his desk and thanked the television technicians whose cameras and microphones had beamed his picture and voice across the country from the Oval Office. Leaving the speech text lying on the desk, he turned and walked toward the glass doors that lead to a colonnade bordering the north and west sides of the White House Rose Garden.

As leader of the 4-P.M.-to-midnight shift of the White House Secret Service detail, I followed to escort him the short distance from the West Wing office to the First Family's living quarters on the second floor of the executive mansion. It was a beautiful spring evening, with flowers on the grounds beginning to bud and soft lights reflecting off the Washington Monument across the South Lawn. But if the President noticed, it wasn't apparent.

Although he had been joking with the TV technicians just prior to his speech, and had delivered the address in his usual style, we had walked only a few feet—just far enough to be out of sight of the office—when he abruptly stopped, leaned against one of the columns, and began to cry. I felt completely helpless.

He had been walking about six feet ahead of me when he stopped. I couldn't see his face in the dim light, but his shoulders heaved as he sobbed and he took a handkerchief from his pocket and held it against his eyes. He stood there for at least a full minute, until he seemed to get control of himself, straightened up, and walked on without ever saying a word to me. I saw him to the elevator that took him up to the second floor, and as the doors closed he stood there alone, staring straight ahead, but seeming completely composed.

It was April 17, 1973, and President Richard M. Nixon had just told the nation that due to "intensive new inquiries" begun March 21, "major developments" had occurred in the Watergate break-in case. He didn't spell out what those developments were, but presidential spokesman Ronald Ziegler would later tell the press that all previous White House statements on what he originally had termed a "third-rate burglary" now were "inoperative."

As I stood there in the darkness that April evening while the President was crying, I wanted to say something to him—to console him, to comfort him, to say, "Mr. President, I believe you." But I couldn't do it. My job was to protect him and nothing more, although I genuinely liked Nixon and at that point I believed he was telling the truth about the Watergate case.

By this time, I had been on the White House Secret Service detail for a little over five years, from President Lyndon Johnson's last year in office through the Nixon administration up to that point. Johnson had not been very well liked by any of the agents on the detail. He treated us as if we were the hired help on his ranch, cursed at us regularly, and was generally a royal pain to deal with.

The contrast in presidential personalities when Nixon came into office was almost shocking. He was courteous and at times even friendly, asking about our families or expressing concern if he heard about some personal problem.

Early in his first term, Nixon was preparing to return to the White House by motorcade from Camp David, the presidential retreat in the Maryland mountains northwest of Washington. Presidents are usually shuttled by helicopter directly from Camp David to the South Lawn of the White House, but on this particular day the weather was too bad to fly. As an agent was moving the presidential limousine up the driveway to the lodge where Nixon was staying, he accidentally blew the horn. Nixon stuck his head out the door and said, "Okay, boys, I'll be out in just a minute."

This type of reaction completely astounded us, because with Johnson, we had been accustomed to waiting anywhere from ten minutes to ten hours for "the boss" to be ready to go. Nixon changed over the years as his image of himself grew with time, but he remained a very private man who often seemed lost in his own thoughts.

One evening in the spring of 1972, when I was the senior agent on duty at the White House, Manolo Sanchez, Nixon's valet, called the Secret Service command post to say that the President wanted to go for a ride to see the Capitol. It was about 8 P.M. I made the necessary arrangements for cars to be brought around to the south entrance and was waiting by the limousine's back door when Nixon came out through the diplomatic entrance. He smiled and nodded toward me, but then walked around the car, stopped, and stood staring out toward the Washington Monument for a long time. Finally, I opened the door and said, "We're ready anytime you are, sir."

Almost obediently, he turned and started around the car to get in. Halfway around, he stopped and said, "Oh, I'm waiting for Timaho," his Irish setter. For a moment, he seemed to have forgotten why he was waiting and had started to follow my comment as though it were an order. After Manolo brought the dog out, we drove up Pennsylvania Avenue toward the Capitol building.

As the senior agent in the motorcade, I was riding in the right front seat of the President's car. On the way to the Capitol,

Nixon leaned up from the backseat and told me he would like to go inside the building to see his old office—the one he had used for the eight years that he had been Vice-President during the Eisenhower administration. There wasn't time to alert the Capitol Police that we were on our way, so we arrived unannounced at the east front entrance. Neither house of Congress was in session and the building was locked and virtually deserted except for the policemen who were on duty. I had to pound on one of the heavy doors to get them to open it and let us in. Nixon walked past the marble statues of famous American statesmen and through the dimly lit hallways toward the Vice-President's office in the Senate wing. When we got there, it was locked, and none of the policemen on duty had the key. They scurried around trying to locate one, but Nixon didn't seem especially concerned about whether or not he got into the office. It seemed that he just wanted to get away from the White House for a time to recall earlier, perhaps happier days in his life.

After walking around the corridors for a while, pausing occasionally to look at a statue or a painting, or to say something to one of the Capitol Police officers, the President was ready to leave. As I recall, he said nothing during the ride back to the White House and appeared to be lost in nostalgia.

I can't remember if this trip up Pennsylvania Avenue took place before or after the break-in at the Democratic National Committee's headquarters in the Watergate complex, in June 1972. It was at about the same time, but it could have been either just before or just after the incident that would finally force Nixon to resign the presidency a little over two years later.

I left the White House detail and was transferred to the Secret Service field office in New Orleans about fourteen months before Nixon resigned, but I saw the beginnings of the collapse of his administration.

That spring of 1973, when I stood alone with Nixon and watched him cry after the Watergate speech, should have been a time of personal and political triumph for the President. He'd been reelected the previous autumn by the largest landslide in the history of American presidential elections, carrying forty-nine states. Just three weeks before his address revealing "major developments" in the Watergate case, the last U.S. combat troops had been withdrawn from Vietnam and the final sixty-seven American prisoners of war had been released in Hanoi. It didn't take long, however, for us to learn the results of the "intensive new inquiries" Nixon had announced in his speech.

On Sunday, April 29, Nixon summoned his two top aides, H. R. (Bob) Haldeman and John Ehrlichman, to Camp David. I was on duty in the Secret Service command post across from Aspen Lodge when they arrived. Both men had been frequent visitors to Camp David over the previous four years, but I had rarely seen them there at the same time. So when they arrived together that afternoon, I had a feeling it was for something more than a routine staff meeting.

When Haldeman and Ehrlichman came out of the lodge after their meeting with Nixon, both of them looked very glum. They were walking side by side to a waiting government car, with the President right behind them. As they stepped off the front porch, Nixon reached up and patted both of them on the back, as if he was trying to cheer them up or bolster their egos. Inside the command post, we didn't know exactly what had taken place during the meeting, but I remember thinking that he had probably asked for their resignations.

I had no strong feelings one way or the other about Ehrlichman, since I rarely dealt with him. But I disliked Haldeman and regarded him as a power-hungry egotist who would do everything in his power to turn the Secret Service into his own private police force were he ever given the chance. I still believe he might have succeeded if those of us on the White House detail hadn't fought him every step of the way for the four years he was White House chief of staff.

The day after the Camp David meeting, the White House press office announced that presidential counsel John Dean had been fired as a result of Watergate and that Haldeman, Ehrlichman, and Attorney General Richard Kleindienst had resigned. In another televised speech to the nation, Nixon praised Haldeman and Ehrlichman and asked that they not be prejudged. He said Kleindienst had quit only because of his personal closeness to others involved in the Watergate investigations. Defense Secretary Elliot L. Richardson was named Attorney General with the authority to appoint a special prosecutor. Nixon denied having any prior knowledge of the break-in that had occurred nearly a year earlier, but he said he accepted responsibility for it and vowed to turn his attention to other, more pressing, national problems.

Two months later, in June 1973, I left the White House detail for the new assignment in New Orleans, so I wasn't in Washington during most of the major political events and congressional hearings that led up to Nixon's resignation from office in August 1974. I don't know how many senior Secret Service officials knew about the secret Oval Office taping system that ultimately led to Nixon's downfall, but none of us who were on duty at the White House day in and day out had any idea that it existed. We sometimes sat around the command post in Room W-16 of the West Wing basement and joked that everything we said about Haldeman or Nixon was probably being recorded. In fact, nothing said in that room was taped, but voice-activated microphones hidden in the Oval Office were recording all conversations there. I have never listened to any of the tapes or read any of the transcripts that were made from them for the congressional hearings on Watergate, but I am sure that my voice is heard on the tapes many times.

Several years after leaving the White House, I found out that the taping system had been installed and maintained in the Oval Office by the Secret Service's Technical Security Division, so obviously there were people in the service who knew about it, but none of them were on the protective detail that worked there every day.

Most Secret Service agents on protective details care little about the political philosophy of those whom they're assigned to guard and even less about politics in general. They are around politicians, often some of the most powerful ones in the world, much of the time and frequently see these men and women at their worst as well as at their best. Above all, agents are professional law-enforcement officers. Their affection for or dislike of a particular president, first lady, or other senior government official they are assigned to protect almost always depends on that individual's personality, sense of humor, and willingness to cooperate when particular security problems demand it, almost never on whether he or she is a Democrat or a Republican, a liberal or a conservative.

After spending twenty years in the Secret Service, I take great pride in the fact that the organization always has remained completely apolitical, and I have the utmost respect for the succession of directors who have kept it so. Should the nonpartisan nature of the service ever change, I am confident that the public would know about it very quickly, because there would be a mass of resignations by agents who would refuse to become anyone's private police force.

Most agents who have served on the White House detail have a kind of love-hate relationship with the job. It is the glamour assignment of the Secret Service—the assignment that can make or break a career. There is constant pressure and stress of a kind that can ruin marriages (as it did mine) and personal lives, but there is also a great deal of satisfaction in being part of one of the most elite law-enforcement units in the world. There are hours and hours of boredom standing guard in a deserted corridor in the middle of the night, interspersed with moments of terror that can be triggered by nothing more than a car backfiring along a presidential motorcade route.

My own years as a member of the White House security force

were very exciting ones, partly because they were some of the most challenging times the Secret Service has ever faced. Nearly every time either President Johnson or President Nixon left the White House, we had to be prepared to do battle with demonstrators opposed to the Vietnam War. But I had my share of the quiet times also.

After Johnson announced in March 1968 that he wouldn't run for reelection, it got very dull around the White House. All of the action shifted to the other presidential candidates and away from Johnson.

I had been assigned to Johnson for only a few weeks when he pulled out of the race. I was young and eager to get into the thick of the election campaign, but now I was relegated to the sidelines.

Johnson loved his LBJ ranch, but the agents assigned to him hated the place. Even when off duty, agents had nothing to do but watch them roll up the sidewalks of Johnson City, Texas, every night. After withdrawing from the presidential election, Johnson went there nearly every weekend. I had wanted to get on the White House detail almost from the day I joined the Secret Service, but now, having finally gotten there, I couldn't get out fast enough.

In August I finally received a temporary assignment to Georgia Governor Lester Maddox. An old-line southern segregationist who had once handed out pickax handles to customers in his Atlanta restaurant to keep blacks out, Maddox had decided he was just what the Democratic party needed to save the country. The only trouble was that, having announced his presidential candidacy, he had no idea what to expect outside of Georgia.

A small contingent of Georgia State Patrol officers was normally assigned to the governor for security. They were a nice bunch of dedicated police officers, but they knew next to nothing about protection work. After he acquired his protective detail, it was a real ego trip for Maddox to drive around Atlanta or to walk around the state capitol building with his own contingent of Secret Service agents. In fact, he seemed to look for reasons to leave his office.

We took Maddox to Chicago a few days before the start of the Democratic National Convention, and it soon became apparent that the only friends he had there were Mayor Richard J. Daley's policemen. At preliminary party meetings leading up to the convention, the delegates often refused to let Maddox even speak. Moving the governor through the streets of Chicago was a real test of a detail's ability to protect someone. We expected, and usually found, trouble wherever we took him.

Nineteen sixty-eight was a year of turbulence in the nation, and civil rights and anti-war groups had been so open in their planning of demonstrations in Chicago during the convention that Mayor Daley had placed the 12,000-man city police force on twelve-hour shifts and 5,600 national guardsmen on duty, with other units standing by. Steel fences were erected around the convention site. In spite of these precautions, or perhaps because of them, violent confrontations between police and demonstrators were daily occurrences, with the police making indiscriminate use of tear gas, Mace, and clubs against demonstrators, reporters, photographers, and bystanders. By the end of the convention, there had been some 668 arrests and as many as 1,000 injuries.

Despite the drastic security measures, it was deemed unsafe for President Johnson to attend, even though a birthday celebration had been planned for him on the second day of the convention. Consequently, the antiwar protesters had to focus their ire on Vice-President Hubert Humphrey, while civil rights demonstrators found a target in Lester Maddox.

Our only advantage was that, while most of the demonstrators in the street knew Maddox's name and politics, most didn't recognize him. But many of them were ready to confront anyone who was important enough to be moving around Chicago sur-

rounded by Secret Service agents, whether they knew who he was
or not. As we were coming out of a hotel one evening, someone
began dropping heavy glass ashtrays from a window on the tenth
floor. After falling a hundred feet, they exploded like hand gre-
nades as they hit the sidewalk all around us. To the governor's
credit, he realized that he was in real danger in Chicago, and he
wouldn't make a move unless we approved. Each time a reporter
asked him if he would be attending a certain function, he turned
to the agent in charge and asked if it would be all right for him to
go. If the agent said it would be okay, Maddox turned back to the
questioner with a somewhat relieved look on his face and said he
would be there. I don't think he even knew why he was going half
the time.

I actually felt a little sorry for Maddox in Chicago, because he
was so far out of his element. He should never have run for President, and I never understood how he failed to realize that no one
would take him seriously. He left Chicago before the convention
itself actually started, and his Secret Service detail was discontinued shortly afterward. The assignment had lasted just two weeks.

Before we returned to Washington, Maddox made us all hon-
orary lieutenant colonels in the "Georgia State Militia" and gave
each of us a souvenir pickax handle. I still have mine, and there is
only one thing wrong with it. "Atlanta" is misspelled. It reads
"Atanta." That seems like an appropriate memento of the governor's brief fling with national politics, but the assignment taught
me a lot about how to react to large-scale demonstrations and
provided a welcome respite from the boredom of the White
House and the LBJ Ranch.

Although antiwar demonstrations, such as those that took
place in the streets of Chicago in 1968, had ended by the spring
of 1973 when I watched the Nixon administration begin to come
apart in the wake of Watergate, they and other pressures had
taken their toll on me. I was emotionally and physically drained.
As a senior agent and assistant shift leader, I was no longer stand-

ing at a post for eight hours, but the night and weekend work continued and the mental stress increased with the additional responsibilities. I felt that I needed a change of pace.

Not long after I left the White House, Secret Service headquarters instituted a policy of rotating agents off the presidential protection detail after three years. The policy remains in effect today, and I believe it is a prudent one. Three years is enough for anyone to live the life that is required of agents assigned to the White House. The stress involved in the job burns people out quickly, and I would go so far as to say there is no job in the world that requires a higher degree of mental alertness or a greater ability to react instantly in any situation.

In my own case, leaving the White House when I did may have saved my life. My first wife and I flew to New Orleans in mid-May 1973 to look for a house prior to moving there. Since we knew we would probably be moving again in three or four years, we spent several days looking for a place that would have good resale value. Nixon was going to the Florida White House at Key Biscayne the following weekend, and normally I would have been on duty and gone with him. I considered trying to get back to Washington in time to make the trip, since another agent would have to replace me and probably lose a weekend when he was supposed to be off duty and at home with his family. However, by the time we found a house we wanted and completed the paperwork involved, it was too late for me to return to Washington before the departure of the detail, so my wife and I decided to spend the night at the lovely Marie Antoinette hotel in the French Quarter before returning home on Friday.

Saturday evening, I was watching television in our family room in the northern Virginia suburbs when an announcer broke in to the regular program to report that a presidential helicopter had crashed in the ocean while en route to an island off the southern Florida coast. The television bulletin didn't say who had been aboard or why the chopper had been going to the island, but I knew that more than likely it had been headed for Grand Cay island, where Nixon's longtime friend Robert H. Abplanalp owned a house. Nixon frequently went there when he was in Key Biscayne. I had been there with him many times.

I immediately called the Secret Service command post at the White House and was told that Nixon was indeed at Abplanalp's house. He had flown there earlier in the day. The helicopter that had crashed had been taking the midnight Secret Service shift to Grand Cay from Key Biscayne to relieve the shift that had been on duty since four o'clock that afternoon.

It was my shift that had gone down in the Atlantic!

There was very little additional information that evening. The next morning, we got word in Washington that Cliff Dietrich, one of the two agents then on temporary assignment to the White House, had been killed in the crash. Other members of the shift and the Army crew chief on the helicopter had been injured, but none of them critically. I still ask myself at times whether I would have been killed if I had been aboard.

The shift leader that night was Chuck Rochner. We have been friends for many years and have occasionally discussed what might have happened had I been there. Since he and I were the number one and number two agents in seniority on the shift, we seldom worked together when the shift had to be split up. Had I been there, I might have taken the men needed to cover the posts around the house on the island while Chuck stayed behind at the command post in Key Biscayne, or vice versa.

Chuck has described to me what happened that night. The chopper they were using was one of several specially equipped Army and Marine Corps helicopters based near Washington for use by the President and other top government officials. When the President is aboard one of them, it is designated Army One or Marine One, as the presidential Boeing 707 is designated Air Force One when he is aboard. Chuck was sitting in the seat where the First Lady usually rides when she is traveling with the

President. He was wearing a set of headphones over which he could hear the military pilots talking to each other as they made what appeared to be a normal and routine approach to the island. One of the pilots was calling out the altitude readings as the chopper descended toward the island's helipad: "Five hundred feet . . . four-fifty . . . four hundred feet . . . three-fifty"—then suddenly the helicopter hit the water.

It was too dark for the pilots to make out the horizon so they had been flying completely by instruments. The altimeter evidently malfunctioned, and they flew nose-first into the ocean. The weight of the twin jet engines mounted on top of the fuselage flipped the helicopter over and it came to rest upside down in the shallow water with only a portion of the tail visible. Within seconds the entire cabin was flooded.

The pilots got out through the broken cockpit windows and swam to the surface. Inside the cabin, however, it was pitch black, and the agents who had been riding there didn't realize that the chopper was upside down. Those sitting in the back swam toward the rear door. A small pocket of air had been trapped in the tail, and most of them were able to reach it. The rear door was hinged on the bottom and opened downward to form steps for boarding, but the helicopter was upside down so the hinges were at the top. To open the rear hatch from outside, the pilots had to dive underwater, release the latch, and then jam their legs into the door to hold it open. By sheer luck, one of the agents inside saw the illuminated dial on one of the pilots' watches through the dark water as they were struggling to get the door open. One by one, those who had been seated in the rear dived down to the opening and slipped through it to the surface as the pilots struggled to hold it open against the current.

Chuck had a harder time getting out. When he got his seat belt off, he swam toward the closest door, which was in the front. But, not realizing that the aircraft was upside down, he was looking for the handle on the wrong side, holding his breath as he

groped about in the murky water. The crew chief was also searching for the front door. Neither of them realized that the front
windows had been broken in the crash.

As he was about to faint from lack of oxygen, Chuck made one
last attempt to locate an exit by swimming to the rear of the helicopter, where the other members of the shift had already gotten
out through the door the pilots were holding open. He came up
in the air pocket, but by this time it had filled with fumes from
the jet fuel that was pouring from the ruptured tanks. Finally realizing that the chopper was overturned in the water and that the
rear door was on the right side instead of the left, Chuck also
managed to get out through it, but he had problems with his
lungs for several years after as a result of breathing the accumu-
lated fumes.

After Chuck got out, the pilot made a final attempt to see if
anyone was still inside. As he reached into the cabin, he felt a leg.
It was the crew chief, who had passed out while searching for the
front door and floated to the air pocket in the rear. The pilots and
members of the detail were able to revive him. The agent who
was killed had been asleep in a seat near Chuck, toward the front
of the helicopter. He had evidently lost consciousness on impact
and drowned. A rescue team found him still strapped into his
seat. One of the men who survived the crash, while physically
uninjured, developed an intense fear of flying immediately afterward. On a flight to Los Angeles shortly after the accident, he got
thoroughly drunk and, when the plane touched down, he had to
be taken off by other agents traveling with him. He was soon
transferred to a job that didn't require travel.

A week after the crash, I rode in another presidential helicopter
from the White House to Camp David with President and Mrs.
Nixon. Since it was an exact duplicate of the one that had gone
down in the Atlantic, I was studying the inside of the cabin, trying to note what I would feel for if I got trapped inside at night
without lights, or if it filled with smoke and I had to get the Presi-

dent and First Lady out in a hurry. I was sitting all the way to the rear in a seat where an agent accompanying the First Family usually rides. The President was in a forward-facing seat with his back toward me, so he couldn't see what I was doing, but Mrs. Nixon was directly across from him in a seat facing me. I glanced at her and saw that she was watching me intently as I studied the inside of the helicopter. She said nothing, but she smiled slightly as my eye caught hers. I believe she was thinking about the crash also, and that she knew exactly what I was doing.

Secret Service agents on protective security details can never stop training or let their guard down for an instant. The pressure never ends because a split-second decision can mean the difference between life and death.

Despite the pressures and problems, the job is tremendously rewarding. Agents assigned to the White House detail see the inner workings of government from a unique perspective. During my twenty years in the Secret Service, I worked with senior officials of five different administrations, two Democratic and three Republican. For the most part, they were dedicated, hardworking men and women who had faults like everyone else.

I wouldn't trade the five years I spent on the White House detail for any other experience I can think of, but neither can I imagine going through another five years like those ever again.

In addition to the mental pressures, there's the sheer physical exhaustion that often accompanies the job. I will cite just one example from dozens any Secret Service agent who has ever been on the White House detail could give. President Nixon decided at the last minute to make a quick stop in Philadelphia once, prior to a weekend trip to Key Biscayne. When I came to work on a Thursday morning I was told that I was the only agent available to head the advance team to Philadelphia. I had only three hours to go back home, pack a bag, and get to the Pentagon heliport to catch a helicopter to Pennsylvania. We left Washington shortly before 1 P.M.; the President would arrive in Philadelphia at noon the next day. By the time I made all of the necessary security arrangements with the local police and the Secret Service field office there—and finished typing my report for the detail that would be arriving with Nixon aboard Air Force One—it was four o'clock on Friday morning. I slept for about an hour after the report went to the White House by Teletype, but then had to get up to begin preparing for the President's arrival.

The brief stop went smoothly, but as soon as the President's plane left the Philadelphia airport for Florida, I had to catch a commercial flight back to Washington, go home to repack for the weekend, and return to National Airport to catch another commercial flight to Miami. I arrived there at 9 P.M. and got to the hotel about 10:30, just in time to change clothes and report to Key Biscayne to take over as leader of the midnight shift.

The agents standing posts around the presidential compound had gone to Florida directly from Washington earlier on Friday, so they had had a chance to get a few hours of sleep before going on duty. But I was the senior agent on duty, and during the night I had to leave the command post several times and walk around outside to keep from nodding off. By the time the shift ended, I had worked from 8 A.M. Thursday until 8 A.M. Saturday with just one hour of sleep.

While this kind of schedule is the exception rather than the rule, it happens almost every time the President or Vice-President decides to take a trip on the spur of the moment. When it does happen, at least a portion of the Secret Service detail directly responsible for protecting the President is often operating at the very limits of human endurance.

CHAPTER 2

Fire at San Clemente

The 1970 congressional elections were just five days away when President Nixon arrived at the "Western White House" in San Clemente, California, shortly before 10 P.M. At every stop Nixon had made during the long day of campaigning, he had been faced with large crowds protesting American involvement in the Vietnam War. As the presidential motorcade passed through San Jose, California, rocks had been thrown at Nixon's limousine. No one was hurt, but the incident shook those of us who were charged with protecting Nixon's life. While we were used to facing angry antiwar protestors nearly everywhere Nixon went during the campaign, this was the first time demonstrators had directly threatened the President in the United States.

It made little difference to members of the White House protective detail which side was right in the turbulent national debate then raging over U.S. foreign policy in Southeast Asia. Our only job was to protect the President from physical harm, no matter what the potential source of danger. I doubt if there was a man on Nixon's detail who agreed with the aims of the antiwar movement, but we frequently went to great lengths to protect the constitutional rights of the demonstrators, occasionally even acting against the wishes of the White House staff, who wanted to use the Secret Service to protect Nixon from political as well as physical harm.

What members of the public often fail to understand and what even veteran Washington observers sometimes forget is that Secret Service agents assigned to the President don't work for the White House staff. They work for the President only in his capacity as Chief Executive. The Secret Service is under the Treasury Department, and in over a century of protecting the country's leaders one of its wisest traditions has been the determination to remain completely apolitical. The majority of agents' personal political views probably fall into the conservative category, although I know of no survey ever taken on the subject and many, like myself, have no strong partisan political convictions one way or the other. Had the Democrats won the White House in 1968, I would probably have found myself on this occasion in 1970 somewhere with Hubert Humphrey as he campaigned for Democratic candidates for Congress.

That night of October 29, 1970, I came on duty at 11 P.M. in the command post at Nixon's San Clemente home as the agent in charge of the overnight shift. It soon became apparent we were going to have more to worry about than antiwar protesters before the night was over.

Following the usual procedure for a shift change, the agent I relieved briefed me on what had happened while he was on duty. Nixon had arrived at 9:51 P.M., he said, and had gone directly to work in his study in the main house, a quarter of a mile from the command post. The night was cold and damp, hardly the kind of weather advertised by the southern California chambers of commerce. Manolo Sanchez, the President's valet, had built a fire in the study's fireplace. The agent I relieved told me the only unusual thing that had occurred during the previous shift after Nixon's arrival at the compound was that smoke from the fire had triggered an alarm in the command post.

Nixon liked having a roaring fire when he worked and would even turn on the air conditioning in warm weather so that he could have one. This had set off smoke alarms before, so it wasn't a particular cause for concern. An officer from the Special Officer Force—a uniformed branch of the Secret Service—who ran the command-post control panel for all alarms in the compound would press a reset switch and the alarm would turn off. It worked in much the same way as a regular home smoke alarm, except that the warning buzzer sounded in the command post instead of inside the President's study.

Our major concern when Nixon was in the study was not the fireplace, but the room's location. It was the place in the compound most vulnerable to outside attack. The San Clemente compound, just off Highway 101 about halfway between Los Angeles and San Diego, covered several acres and was comprised of half a dozen or so buildings, a private beach, a swimming pool, and a helipad. The entire estate was enclosed by a brick wall, and uniformed officers manned a checkpoint at the entrance gate at all times when Nixon was President. The main house was a Spanish-style quadrangle with white adobe walls, a red tile roof, and an open courtyard in the center. It was one story except for the study, which had been added on above the dining room on the southwest corner sometime after the completion of the original building. This room could be reached only by an outside staircase leading from the interior courtyard.

The southwest corner of the house faced the Pacific Ocean, but a fence just twenty-five yards away divided the compound from a public beach and the streets of a residential neighborhood. The fence was the closest point to the house from which an attack on the President could have been launched. Spotlights were trained on it throughout the night, and when Nixon was in the house, an agent was always on duty at the corner beneath the study. Still, I often wondered as I stood at that post how I would stop a well-coordinated assault if it ever came.

Less than half an hour into my shift, at about 11:25 P.M., I was relaxing in the command post located midway between the main house and the front gate of the compound, enjoying the luck of drawing the midnight shift for the last few days before the election. The President had left the study and crossed the courtyard to his bedroom, where he was safely asleep. Mrs. Nixon was on a campaign tour of her own in another part of the country and wouldn't return that night. With Nixon in bed for most of my shift, I wouldn't have to deal with demonstrators as my fellow agents had been doing most of that day.

The Secret Service isn't like a private company in which the newest employees work the graveyard shift until they acquire enough seniority to work days. Experienced agents must be on duty all the time, along with younger men (and today, women agents also serve as "post standers" guarding the area immediately around the President). Shifts are rotated every two weeks, so that the same agents don't have to work nights all the time. Midnight duty is usually the least popular of the three shifts, but just before an election when a president is on the campaign trail most of the time, it has its advantages.

My reverie in the command post was interrupted by the buzzing of a smoke alarm from the house, this time from the dining room beneath the study. Since I knew there was no fireplace in that room, I wondered if there was a short circuit somewhere in the alarm system. When the officer on duty pressed the reset switch on the control panel, the alarm stopped, but it went off again a few seconds later. Just then, I heard one of the agents manning a post outside say something over the radio about an unusual "fog" beginning to settle in over the main house. In less than a minute, another alarm sounded.

I became very concerned and told the special officer on duty with me to call Fina Sanchez, Manolo's wife, and ask her to check the house. All of the security posts manned by agents were outside, but Manolo and Fina, who had worked for the Nixons for many years, had their own quarters next to the kitchen and across the courtyard from Nixon's bedroom. Within seconds, Fina was back on the phone, screaming, "Call the fire department! Call the fire department! The house is full of smoke!"

As the assistant shift leader on duty with me in the command post dialed the San Clemente Fire Department, I began issuing orders to all the agents and uniformed officers on duty. The first concern, of course, was the President. The agent nearest his bedroom advised me over the radio that he would get Nixon up and to a safe place outside the house. Another agent would move so he could cover both his own post and that of the man going inside to wake the President. It wasn't the job of the agents standing post to deal with the fire. Their duty was to get Nixon away from the danger and to maintain a security screen around him.

Since Mrs. Nixon was away and I knew Manolo and Fina were up and safe, we didn't have to worry about anyone else being inside. But obviously we had to contend with the fire.

Five years earlier, as a rookie agent attending the Treasury Department law-enforcement school in Washington, I had spent one afternoon at the city's fire-training center watching a demonstration of fire-fighting techniques given by the District of Columbia Fire Department. That was the total extent of my "training" as a fireman. I knew there was a fire hose on a wall diagonally across the interior courtyard from the dining room, but I had never seen it used and wasn't certain it worked, although I assumed it did. I assigned an officer to stand by it when we arrived at the house, and told others to collect all the fire extinguishers and bring them to the dining room when we got there. We then gathered up all the fire extinguishers in the command post.

Because of the size of the compound, we used golf carts to get around. That night, one of them was sitting in front of the command post. We all piled onto it and started for the house. I have often thought since then that we must have looked like something out of an old Keystone Kops movie—five or six grown men in coats and ties or crisp police uniforms hanging on to a golf cart, charging up the President's driveway with fire extinguishers at the ready. Well, "charging" may not be exactly the right word: The golf cart was so badly overloaded that I am sure we could have run to the house much faster than it got us there.

At any rate, when we arrived, one of the officers and I went into the dining room. It was filled with smoke, but I could see flames in the wall next to the door through a recessed stereo speaker. Long steel rods had been driven through the bottom of the fireplace in the study above, into the wall's supporting timbers. The rods had conducted so much heat from the President's earlier fire that they had ignited the old, dry wood inside the wall.

I told the officer with me to take the cover off the speaker box so we could get some water into the wall. He began trying to take out the screws that held the mesh cover in place, but was having trouble turning them. By this time, the agents and officers outside had uncoiled the fire hose and dragged it across the courtyard. Finally, I told the officer with me to "knock the goddamn box into the wall" so I could get some water on the fire.

So there I stood in the President's dining room, a civil servant with absolutely no experience as a fire fighter, wearing one of my best suits and holding the hose, when someone outside turned on the water. I heard it come rumbling through the hose, which was stretched nearly a hundred feet across the courtyard. When the pressure hit the nozzle I was holding, it knocked me back several feet, spraying the furniture, the curtains, the carpet—just about everything in the room except the fire in the wall.

I regained my footing, got control of the hose, and stood there filling the wall with a stream of water until it occurred to me that I didn't know for certain where the President was and if he was safe. The thought ran through my head that the fire could have been set to divert our attention. As the shift leader, I was the senior Secret Service agent present. While I trusted the men under me to do their jobs, I was the person directly responsible for the President's safety.

I edged toward the dining room door, keeping the water trained on the burning wall, but I couldn't see outside because of the smoke. Finally I reached the door. Although I don't recall using the exact language, the agents who were outside claim that my head emerged briefly through the smoke as I yelled, "Who's got the fucking President?"

I recall vividly the voice that answered.

"I'm right here," Nixon said. "Everything is fine."

The two agents with the President almost collapsed with laughter at my less than proper comment, with Nixon standing just a few feet outside the door I yelled through. The agents on post had urged him to go to the guesthouse across the driveway from the main house, but he didn't want to leave until he found out what had happened.

We were normally pretty careful about our language around the President and any other dignitaries we were protecting but, as the Watergate tapes later revealed, Nixon was no stranger to salty language himself. He never said a word about my indiscreet phrase during the fire. I'm not sure he even noticed it.

When the volunteer firemen from San Clemente arrived, Nixon was standing at the front door waiting for them. We had the fire out by this time and I walked across the courtyard just in time to see the President, wearing a dark blue bathrobe that came down to his knees, black socks, and black shoes, standing there shaking hands with each fireman who came running up to the door. For the second time that night, it was like viewing a scene from an old, silent movie. The stunned firemen, dressed for action in helmets, boots, and heavy raincoats, were running into each other as the President of the United States stood there in his bathrobe greeting them with his hand outstretched.

"Thank you for coming, thank you for coming," Nixon told

each man, not missing the chance to get in one more bit of campaigning before the day ended.

Despite these comic scenes, the fire was serious. The chief of the San Clemente volunteers told us that if we hadn't taken quick action, the house might have been destroyed.

As the firemen were cleaning up, Nixon asked me about the damage. I told him there was very little from the fire itself, since it had been contained in the one wall in the dining room, but there was quite a bit of smoke and water damage. I didn't mention that I was responsible for most of the water damage.

"How about the dining room?" the President asked as we walked across the courtyard so he could have a look for himself.

"Quite a bit there, Mr. President," I said, explaining how the fire appeared to have started inside the wall.

"And the living room?" he asked.

"There too, sir," I replied.

The living room was next to the dining room on the side of the house facing the ocean, and heavy smoke had filled that entire wing. There was a breezeway leading to the swimming pool between the living room and Nixon's bedroom, so he hadn't been in any serious danger from either the fire or the smoke.

After walking through the damaged rooms to see for himself what I was talking about, Nixon had only one comment as we stood there looking at the mess.

"Oh," he said, "Pat's going to be pissed off when she sees this."

After an investigation of the fire and our response to it, I got a letter of commendation from James J. Rowley, then director of the Secret Service, but not before the other agents on the shift had some fun. One of them stole a sheet of paper from a memo pad with the heading "From the Desk of Bob Haldeman" and typed a very formal memo to Bob Taylor, the agent in charge of the White House Secret Service detail. The phony memo, left where I would be sure to see it, demanded a meeting with Taylor as soon as possible to discuss the "foul language" being used around the President by one of his agents.

Dealing with incidents like the fire is a side of the Secret Service that the public almost never hears about because rarely does the organization—or an individual agent—get credit for its accomplishments at such times. What really happened is often known only inside the Secret Service. It can be frustrating to have acted in a professional manner and to have done everything that could have been done under the circumstances, and then to see someone else get all the credit. But that is something every Secret Service agent soon learns to live with, and it happened to my shift the morning after the fire at San Clemente.

Shortly after midnight, with the fire out and the excitement over, we took Nixon to the guesthouse in the compound and adjusted the watch posts to provide maximum protection there rather than around the main house. I then spent the rest of the night dealing with the Secret Service brass who descended on the Western White House to investigate what had happened. By the next morning, the White House staff had gotten into the act.

It was decided that Nixon should go to the firehouse in San Clemente to thank the men there for "saving" his house. White House Press Secretary Ron Ziegler notified the television networks and newspaper reporters who were traveling with Nixon that the President would change his campaign schedule so that he could go to the firehouse. While this was an appropriate gesture, since the firemen had gotten to the house in just over ten minutes from the time we had called them, it also guaranteed that Nixon would be seen on national television that evening thanking ordinary firemen—instead of federal agents in three-piece suits—for saving his home.

In the White House press office, this is known as a "photo opportunity."

Bob Taylor, our direct supervisor, had ordered those of us who had been on duty and actually put out the fire to stand by to go to

the firehouse with the President. We later found out that Haldeman had overruled Taylor, saying he didn't give a damn who had
put out the fire; the local firemen, not the Secret Service, were
going to get the credit.

The October 30, 1970, edition of the *Los Angeles Times* carried a ten-paragraph story about the incident with a one-column
headline reading FIRE ROUTS NIXON FROM HIS HOME IN SAN CLE-
MENTE. Quoting Ziegler, the story said the fire had been discovered by Fina Sanchez. The only mention of the Secret Service
was in the last paragraph. It said we had called the fire department. However, as it turned out, the fire ended up helping my
career anyway.

The first senior Secret Service official to arrive at the Western
White House after the fire had been Pat Boggs, the assistant
director in charge of protective details. Normally, he didn't travel
with us, but he happened to be in California that night. At the
time, Boggs was the second or third most powerful official in the
service. The assistant directors for protection and investigations
rank right behind the director in the organizational pecking order.
There is a deputy director, but he usually has less influence than
the assistant directors because his duties are primarily administrative.

About three months before the fire, I had asked for a transfer
to a field office. I had been on the White House detail for two
and a half years and on a three-shift rotation schedule for five
years; I was ready, I felt, to get back to a more normal nine-to-
five job.

There are over sixty Secret Service field offices around the
country and agents assigned to them mainly carry out the mission
for which the service was originally established, the protection of
U.S. currency against counterfeiting. This consists primarily of
basic police work. While there is sometimes night duty involving
investigations or stakeouts, agents in the field offices usually work
fairly regular hours. My wife and I, by then with two small chil-

dren, hadn't decided in which part of the country we wanted to live, so I put in a request for a transfer to an unspecified field office. Agents coming off the White House detail usually get their choice of assignments.

A few days after my request went in, Bob Taylor called me into his office and asked me to stay on his detail. He said that he needed my experience and that if I stayed at the White House, he would see to it that I got promoted to Grade 13, one level higher in the civil service, which would mean higher pay. His argument was persuasive and I withdrew my transfer request.

Taylor was completely dedicated to the Secret Service. He had won the Treasury Department's Exceptional Service Award, the service's highest medal at that time, for his performance on Nixon's vice-presidential detail. Nixon had insisted on going ahead with a "goodwill" tour of South America in April 1958 despite Central Intelligence Agency reports that there might be an attempt on his life. At that time, the Vice-President didn't have a regular Secret Service detail, but agents were assigned to him when he traveled. Taylor was on the detail that took Nixon to Uruguay, Peru, and Venezuela. There were mild anti-Nixon demonstrations in Montevideo, Uruguay, and when the Vice-President reached Lima, Peru, rocks were thrown at the motorcade, hitting Nixon and some of the agents, although no one was seriously injured.

The real trouble came in Caracas, Venezuela's capital, as the CIA had predicted it would. Thousands of anti-American demonstrators were waiting for Nixon at the airport. The noise of the mob was so loud that the welcoming nineteen-gun salute couldn't be heard over its roar. As the motorcade left the airport for Nixon to lay a wreath at the tomb of Simón Bolívar, a stream of rocks and bottles showered the cars from all directions. A few blocks from Bolívar's tomb, a truck blocked the motorcade's route entirely, forcing it to stop. There were a total of ten agents in the motorcade and for approximately twelve minutes they got no help from Venezuelan security forces as the demonstrators rocked the cars, attempting to turn them over. Finally, a contingent of Venezuelan troops arrived and led the motorcade to the American Embassy. Nixon never forgot Taylor and the other men who were with him that harrowing day in Caracas.

Well over six feet tall and darkly handsome, Taylor looked like the public's image of a Secret Service agent. Everyone on the White House detail respected him, but he had a lightning temper and wasn't one to ingratiate himself with anyone, including the President, the White House staff, and the Secret Service hierarchy. At the time I wanted to leave his detail, Taylor was in the midst of a power struggle with headquarters over who had control of agents assigned to the White House. This was to be my first, but certainly not my last, encounter with the service's internal politics, something the public and even members of Congress rarely hear about.

Taylor had assured me that I would be getting my GS-13 grade the next time promotions were made, but when the list of promotions came out, I wasn't on it, although four other White House agents who were beneath me in seniority were there. I was hurt and confused, not to mention more than a little angry, when I saw the list. I asked for an appointment with Taylor to discuss it. When I got to his office, he was burning mad. He said he was sorry I had been passed over and told me the reason was that headquarters was trying to show him that it—not he—would make all decisions concerning members of the detail.

"I'll make you a promise, Denny," he told me. "No one else will be promoted on this detail until you get your thirteen."

Without warning, I was suddenly in the middle of a fight so far above my level in the bureaucracy that I hadn't even known it was going on. I had no idea who was going to win, but I could guess who a sure loser was likely to be. I could see Taylor going to battle with headquarters over me, and headquarters saying, "McCarthy will never get promoted," just to prove a point to Taylor.

I asked Bob to back off and let me go directly to Boggs, the assistant director for protection, to find out why I had been passed over for promotion. Taylor gave me permission to do so, and I made an appointment. When I arrived at his office at Secret Service headquarters three blocks from the White House, Boggs was cordial and asked what he could do for me. I explained politely that I had wanted a transfer a few weeks earlier, but had withdrawn my request because Taylor asked me to stay and told me I would be on the next promotion list if I did. I added that I didn't think the agents who had been promoted were any more qualified than I, although I had nothing against any of them personally and was happy to see them getting ahead.

When I finished, I got a cock-and-bull story about how the others had been promoted ahead of me because they had scored just slightly better than I in their evaluations. It sounded fine, but anyone who has been in the Secret Service longer than a week knows that the system doesn't work that way. Nevertheless I had to sit and listen to Boggs's line. If I had said what I really thought, my career would have been as good as over then and there. So I played the game, and asked what I was doing wrong and how I could improve myself.

"You're doing a fine job, Denny," the assistant director said, "and there's no problem. It's just a matter of time until you're promoted."

The San Clemente fire occurred less than three weeks after that meeting. As I was standing outside the damaged dining room, explaining to Boggs how we had put the fire out, Fina Sanchez came running over and began telling him what had happened. She said that I had done a great job, that I had saved the house and should get a promotion for it. She had no idea of the recent clash between Taylor and headquarters, but it almost looked as if I had staged the whole scene. From the look on Boggs's face as Fina chattered on, I'm sure he too was recalling our recent meeting in Washington.

Two months later, I was promoted to GS-13 and, due to my

seniority, was assigned permanently to the number two spot of assistant shift leader. Therefore, for most of the next two and a half years, when I was on duty, I was almost always the person directly responsible for the safety of the President of the United States.

Whether the President is going across the street or around the world, an elaborate security network is in place before he ever leaves the White House. It sometimes takes weeks of planning and travel to make the necessary arrangements for overseas trips or extended swings through the United States. From the winter of 1971 until the late spring of 1973, when I left the White House detail, nearly every hour I worked I was acting shift leader unless I was traveling ahead of the President doing advance work. The job entails tremendous responsibility and pressure as well as incredibly long hours of continuous work.

Psychiatrists who have studied the Secret Service have compared the stress on agents guarding the President to that faced by fighter pilots in combat. The White House Secret Service detail is one of the few jobs in the world where there is absolutely no margin for error. Every agent on the detail must be willing to trade his life for the President's. It comes with the territory.

During my twenty years in the Secret Service, I helped protect five Presidents—from Lyndon Johnson to Ronald Reagan. I was a member of the White House detail for five years, from 1968 to 1973. During most of this period the country was deeply divided over the civil rights movement, the Vietnam War, and, after 1972, Watergate. The anger and frustration felt by millions of Americans at the policies of the Johnson and Nixon administrations were directed at the two men personally. We had to be ready to do battle with hundreds, sometimes thousands, of our fellow citizens every time the President left the White House.

We felt we were caught in the middle of a political storm. Despite the pressures we were under, I don't know of a single instance when the Secret Service violated the rights of anyone demonstrating against government policy, during that time or since. If someone arrives at the site of a presidential appearance carrying a sign attached to a baseball bat or something else that can be used as a weapon, a Secret Service agent can, and will, take it away from him or her. But if someone holds up a sign reading REAGAN SUCKS or BABY KILLER—a favorite of the militant anti-abortion groups during the Ford and Carter administrations—the Secret Service won't interefere. Agents are there to protect the President's body, not his ego or his political standing. That was what I was doing early one afternoon in late March 1981, outside the VIP entrance to the Washington Hilton Hotel.

CHAPTER 3

An Assassin Strikes

March 30, 1981, was just another routine day until John W. Hinckley, Jr., started shooting at the President.

I had been assigned to the protective intelligence section of the Secret Service's Washington field office for five months. The section's primary duty is to keep tabs on potential threats to the President and other senior government officials. It is an important job within the service, but not usually a particularly exciting one. Mostly it consists of conducting background checks and following up on bits and pieces of information on individuals who could pose a threat to anyone the Secret Service is protecting.

I had arrived at my office in the Secret Service headquarters building three blocks from the White House at about 9 A.M. after the usual forty-five minutes of stop-and-go driving from my house in the Virginia suburbs. My partner for the day was a young black agent named Danny Spriggs, who, after a promising college football career, had been drafted as a defensive back by the Dallas Cowboys before he joined the Secret Service. We would be the

PI (protective intelligence) team for President Reagan's speech that day at the Washington Hilton. Normally there would have been a second, two-man team working with us, but due to illness and other demands on the office that day there were no other agents available to form a second team.

My first check of the day was to find out if any demonstrations were planned in or around the hotel while the President would be there. Apparently, there were none. Reagan had been in office just a little over two months, and his popularity with the American people was still very high. I then checked to see if there were any active threats against Reagan by people we call "lookouts"— individuals who are considered extremely dangerous. The Secret Service's Office of Protective Intelligence uses computers to keep tabs on approximately 40,000 individuals and groups that might pose a threat to the President. Of these, about 350 are regarded as serious threats that must be watched carefully if they are in the vicinity of the President. They are the lookouts, the ones with a history either of violence or of mental illness.

Hinckley wasn't on this list, because he had never before directly threatened a president, although records later revealed that he had been arrested in Tennessee for trying to board a commercial airliner in Nashville with three pistols in his possession while President Carter was speaking a few miles from the aiport. Senior Secret Service officials said that the FBI had never informed the service of this arrest.

"At a minimum, we would have interviewed him and possibly placed him on a suspect list," former Secret Service Director H. Stuart Knight later told a congressional investigating committee. But for whatever reason, Hinckley wasn't on the list of people considered potentially dangerous to the President when I made my check just three hours before he shot Reagan.

Every year, the Secret Service investigates about fourteen thousand threats against the President, Vice-President, and other federal officials it is assigned to protect. Most of these cases are nothing more than some guy sounding off in a bar that the President is such a jerk, someone ought to shoot him. But even this type of remark is taken seriously and investigated if it is overheard by a law-enforcement officer or private citizen and reported to the service. There is a Secret Service field-office telephone number inside the front cover of every phone book printed in the United States. Some four hundred people are arrested every year for threatening the President.

At about ten o'clock on the morning of the shooting, I called Bill Green, the White House Secret Service advance agent, who was in charge of overall security for the day. We discussed the lack of any intelligence, and he gave me the basic information on Reagan's speech—the group he was addressing, how many people were expected, and so on.

There was to be a briefing at the Hilton at noon for the agents who would be standing posts around the hotel while the President was there, Bill said. I told him I would be there to advise them if any intelligence matters were to develop. About twenty-five agents were scheduled for the event. The Secret Service goes through this procedure every time the President leaves the White House to make an appearance in Washington. He doesn't go anywhere until a security screen is in place, and the precautions became even greater after Hinckley's attempt on the President's life and the dramatic increase in terrorist attacks against Americans in the years after 1981.

I drove up Connecticut Avenue to the Hilton in a government car, arriving shortly after 11 A.M. I walked the route the President would be taking through the hotel, then went to the room where the agent briefing would be conducted. In the briefing, Green went over the President's schedule and the post assignments for the agents who were working the speech. I then gave the intelligence briefing, basically saying that we had nothing unusual to report.

It looked as if Reagan's appearance would be routine in every way.

The President or Vice-President addresses a group in the Hilton's main ballroom almost every week. It is one of the largest rooms in Washington, and many national organizations use it for conventions. Most of the Secret Service agents in Washington know every inch of the area because they are there so often.

After the briefing, Danny Spriggs and I accompanied Green as he took all the agents on his team around the building to show them their assignments. By doing so, we would know exactly where they all were in case they called us to come and interview someone who was causing a problem. It is the PI team's job to determine if there is a possible threat to the President and to make the arrest if there is probable cause.

By the time the four thousand guests began arriving for the speech, Danny and I were standing on either side of the ballroom's main entrance to observe as many people as we could when they came in. I checked the coats of a couple of people when I noticed bulges that could have been weapons, but I found nothing. After the shooting, the service began using metal detectors like those used at airports to check guests at presidential appearances. It has now become a status symbol in Washington to attend a dinner or reception where guests have to go through one of these detectors, a greater status symbol to give a party where your guests have to go through one, and the ultimate in status to be able to go anywhere in the city without ever having to pass through a metal detector.

On the day of the shooting, the crowd was very orderly and businesslike, so I didn't anticipate any problems during the speech. The President was due to arrive at the hotel at 1:50 P.M. for the scheduled two o'clock address. The members of the White House advance team, still relatively new at their jobs, had been a little late in opening the doors to the ballroom. I was somewhat concerned that not all of the guests would be inside by the time Reagan got there. Danny and I had to stay at the ballroom entrance until everyone was inside, but we also needed to be at the VIP entrance to the hotel when the motorcade from the

White House arrived. The problem was solved for us as the flow of guests going into the ballroom slowed to a trickle. We got a call on the radio requesting that the PI team report to the VIP entrance. This meant there was some kind of problem at the entrance where Reagan was due to arrive momentarily.

"I'll bet you ten to one it's Mickey Crowe," I told Danny as we walked through the hotel. He declined my bet, saying I was probably right. Crowe had been at every presidential appearance I had worked for the past several weeks. He usually shouted some antinuclear slogan when Reagan arrived and departed, but he had never made any physical move toward the President. So long as he made no such move, he was doing nothing more than exercising his constitutional rights as far as the Secret Service was concerned. Mickey was well over six feet tall. When Danny and I got to the hotel entrance, I could see his head towering over the other people around him. When he saw me, I gave him a little wave. He smiled and waved back. I shook my finger at him, as if to say, "Be a good boy and don't cause any trouble."

Danny and I then walked over to the senior agent at the entrance to see what the problem was. Sure enough, he wanted to advise us that he had spotted a potential troublemaker in the crowd. He pointed to Mickey. I told him we would keep an eye on Crowe, but we didn't expect any trouble from him. I didn't want to interview Mickey at that time, because I knew he would start talking to me and distract me during the President's arrival.

We had no idea that the real problem, Hinckley, was standing only a few feet from Crowe at this time.

Pictures taken during the arrival show that Hinckley was in the group of fifteen to twenty people who were standing behind the television cameras, along with Mickey. Had this been a designated press area, only reporters and technicians with credentials issued by the Secret Service would have been allowed there, but it wasn't reserved for the media. There was simply a rope stretched across the sidewalk about twenty-five to thirty feet from the hotel's T Street entrance. The network camera crews assigned to record the President's arrival and departure always set up there because it is the best place to get the pictures they need of him entering and leaving the hotel. Reporters and camera crews actually covering the speech were already inside the ballroom.

There was only one reason the crews were outside: to have their cameras rolling in case someone took a shot at the President. Previous assassination attempts had made the arrangement standard procedure. The networks call it "the body watch."

Just before the motorcade arrived from the White House, Danny and I walked around behind the rope so we would be close to Mickey and could respond quickly in case he made an unusual move. There is no way to know for sure, but this may have been the reason that Hinckley didn't try to shoot Reagan when he arrived at the hotel. Hinckley must have recognized us as Secret Service agents, and we were very close to him.

When Reagan got out of his car, he went straight into the hotel and directly to the speaker's podium in the main ballroom, where he was greeted with a standing ovation. Danny and I followed him to mingle with the large crowd of people who were standing around the edges of the huge, oval-shaped room. We moved around constantly during the speech, circulating through the crowd looking for anything unusual. There was nothing out of the ordinary.

After the President finished speaking, he left the ballroom through a side entrance and walked to a holding room where he would wait briefly before leaving the hotel to return to the White House. This too is standard procedure. It not only gives the President time to confer with his staff, meet with people, or make phone calls, if necessary, but also allows any security personnel who need to change locations time to do so.

As soon as Reagan left the ballroom, Danny and I left through another side door leading into the same hallway so we could get ahead of the President and be outside to look the crowd over before he came out. As we reached the exit, I was walking slightly ahead of Danny and went through the door first. I looked to the left and saw the same group of twenty or so people still standing behind the television camera crews. When Danny saw me move toward that area, he went to the right. We didn't have to speak to each other. We moved instinctively to cover open areas.

The rope behind which the cameramen and a small group of spectators were standing began at a wall of the hotel, but it came to an end near the driveway in which the presidential motorcade was parked. Since someone could walk around it into the driveway, I went to that side of the crowd and positioned myself in line with the cameras, facing away from the doors through which the President would walk in a minute or two. It would be difficult for anyone to get through the camera crews and across the rope, but if someone tried to rush out of the crowd, I could quickly move across in front of the cameramen to stop him.

Little did I know just how quickly I would have to move.

As the shots rang out, my reaction was more instinctive than conscious. Had I been able to see the gun when Hinckley pulled it from his coat, I believe I would have been able to reach him before he got a shot off. That extra second or two could have made the difference, but since my line of vision was blocked by the cameras, I didn't know the gun was there until after he had fired the first shot.

Hinckley was standing near the hotel wall, behind one or two rows of people. The sound of his shots recorded by the television crews shows that he emptied the six bullets in his pistol in just under two seconds. I started to dive in his direction as he fired the second shot and landed on his back on the sixth. The impact of my body caused the last shot to go high and strike a building across the street.

Hinckley may have rushed his shots because of where I was standing. It may simply have been fear and anxiety about what he was doing that caused him to empty the gun as fast as he could pull the trigger, but he probably knew there was a Secret Service agent standing just six to eight feet away.

As Hinckley and I hit the pavement, other agents and Washington police officers piled on top of us. Hinckley was pinned down and couldn't move. His arms were stretched out in front of him about a foot apart and two agents held each arm. I had difficulty getting my handcuffs from my belt because of all the people piled on top of me. When I reached the handcuffs, I snapped one on Hinckley's left wrist, but I had to yell at the men who were holding his right arm to ease up so I could pull it close enough to his left to get the other cuff on.

It was a struggle to get to my feet and to get Hinckley up. As I was pulling him to his feet, I saw that an older man from the crowd of spectators had somehow gotten into the pile and had both hands around Hinckley's neck, trying to choke him.

"Let him go," I yelled twice.

When he continued to choke my prisoner, I gave him a quick jab to the jaw with my right elbow, knocking him away. I didn't mean to hurt the old man, but I was concerned about keeping Hinckley safe in all the confusion. We had no way of knowing whether Hinckley had acted alone or was part of a conspiracy, so it was essential that we be able to question him when we reached a safer place.

Nearly everyone at the scene was shouting or screaming commands at one another, but my responsibility had shifted from protecting the President to protecting my prisoner.

As I had been making my dive toward Hinckley, Jerry Parr, chief of the White House Secret Service detail, and his assistant, Ray Shaddick, were thrusting the President into the back seat of the waiting limousine. Ironically, this was when Reagan was hit, as a bullet ricocheted off the limousine and struck him in the chest. Had Parr and Shaddick not reacted as quickly as they did, Reagan probably wouldn't have been hit, but the two White House agents did exactly what they were supposed to do—get him into the car and away from the scene as fast as possible. Before I had the handcuffs on Hinckley, Reagan was already away from the hotel.

Not knowing at first that the President had been shot, Parr ordered Drew Unrue, the limousine driver, to go straight to the White House because it is the most secure place in Washington. Seconds after the motorcade pulled away, however, Reagan complained to Parr that he was having difficulty breathing, and he started coughing up bright red blood. Knowing this meant the President had a lung injury, Parr changed his mind and took the motorcade directly to the emergency entrance of George Washington University Hospital, five blocks west of the White House.

By the time I got Hinckley to his feet, Danny was back at my side. I had my right arm locked through Hinckley's left arm and Danny was in the same position on his right side. I knew we had to get him out of there fast.

We have to keep him alive, I kept repeating to myself.

As we began moving Hinckley toward a police car, another citizen came running toward us, cursing. I hit him hard, and he staggered back. He didn't approach us again. By this time I was feeling a little numb, but I wasn't about to let anyone get near my prisoner. When we reached the nearest police car, the back door was jammed and the officers standing by it were unable to get it open.

"Let's move him to the other car," I yelled to Danny as I looked around and saw another blue-and-white squad car drive up while the officers were struggling with the door on the first car.

As we started for the second car, a man I didn't recognize as a Secret Service agent got in our way, and I later saw on the television tapes that I knocked him aside also. I jumped into the backseat of the police car, pulling Hinckley in behind me, followed by Danny. The television tapes show that it was two and a half minutes from the time the shooting started until we had Hinckley into the car and away from the scene. It took the presidential motorcade just three minutes to get Reagan to the hospital.

I told Officer Leon Swain, who was driving the squad car, to go straight to Washington Metropolitan Police Department headquarters.

It was quiet in the car, except for the scream of the siren, as we drove through the moderate afternoon traffic in downtown Washington. My mouth was completely dry, and I remember wishing I had a drink of water. My mind was teeming with all sorts of thoughts, most of them concerning the Kennedy assassination, though at the time I had no idea if Hinckley's shots had hit anyone or not. In the confusion following the shooting, I hadn't seen that three people had been left wounded.

All I knew was that I had custody of a prisoner who had just fired shots at the President of the United States, and it was now my duty to protect both his life and his constitutional rights.

Hinckley's wrists were handcuffed in front of him. Normally, I would have handcuffed his arms behind his body, but there hadn't been time in the rush to get him away from the hotel. Since we hadn't had time to search him, we didn't know if he had any other weapons, so Danny and I pinned his hands above his head against the wire screen between the front and back seats of the car.

As we drove toward police headquarters, Hinckley turned to me and said he thought his right wrist was broken. He asked me to loosen the handcuffs. I looked at him and for the first time saw him in color. I noticed that he had sandy hair and a light complexion. It was the first time that I had looked at his face.

"You're fucking lucky that was the only thing that was broken," I told him. I had no intention of loosening the handcuffs or taking my hand off his arm until we could search him properly. He didn't ask if the President had been shot or anything else about the incident. He was silent for the rest of the trip to the police station.

Recalling that Lee Harvey Oswald had been shot inside police headquarters in Dallas after he had killed President Kennedy in 1963, I asked Officer Swain to radio his headquarters and have the basement entrance cleared of all people except uniformed officers. He made the call, but when we arrived at the police station there was no one in sight, not even any uniformed officers. As we got out of the car, I took out my revolver and held it in a raised position as we rushed Hinckley into the building. It was the only time during the entire day that I had a gun in my hand. I had no idea what to expect. We surprised the officers in charge of the lockup section at police headquarters when we walked in. Despite the radio call, they hadn't gotten word yet that we were bringing in a prisoner who had just shot at the President.

I asked if there was an empty cell I could use. They pointed in the direction of the cellblock. We moved Hinckley into the block and pushed him up against a wall. I took his handcuffs off and we spread-eagled him against the wall. I advised him of his rights as Danny started to search him, taking everything out of his pockets. He had no other weapons, and he said he understood his rights. The cellblock supervisor came in. I asked him which cell we could put Hinckley in. He told me to take my choice. They were all empty.

After we placed Hinckley in a cell, I stood outside it and watched him while Danny and the city officers on duty took his possessions into another room to inspect and catalogue them. I didn't want to leave Hinckley alone for even a minute, because I didn't know if he would try to harm himself, and I wanted to be sure no one else would try to harm him.

Word spread quickly through the building that we had a prisoner in the cellblock who had tried to shoot the President. Soon, two plainclothes officers from the homicide section came down to assist us. They suggested that we move Hinckley upstairs to an interview room where he would be safer. When we got him to the room, we handcuffed him to a table. He hadn't complained any further about his wrist being broken, but we put the handcuff that was attached to the table on his other wrist. From time to time over the two hours that he remained in the interview room, he moved his right arm over so he could rub his wrist with his left hand. I assumed he was having some pain in his arm, possibly from hitting the pavement when I tackled him, but he didn't complain about it again.

At 3:10 P.M. Officer Ed Meyers of the Washington police came into the room to read Hinckley his rights, letting Hinckley read along with him. I remember the time because Meyers checked it with me so he could record it on Hinckley's "rights form," a legal document certifying that anyone who has been arrested was advised of his constitutional rights as required by federal law. Again, Hinckley said he understood his rights.

Officer Meyers then asked Hinckley if he wanted to talk about the shooting. Hinckley said he would rather not talk until he could see his lawyer. We asked him where his attorney's office was located and how we could get in touch with him. He said his lawyer was in Dallas. Meyers then asked Hinckley what his own name was, but he was reluctant to give it to us until he talked with his attorney. We told him that we couldn't contact anyone until we had some basic information about him.

"My name is John W. Hinckley, Jr.," he said. That was the first time that I heard his name.

Hinckley told us he was from Evergreen, Colorado. He said he had just arrived in Washington the day before, Sunday, March 29. When we asked him where he was staying, Hinckley couldn't remember the name of the hotel, but said he thought it was the "Plaza" or something like that. Since there is no Plaza Hotel in Washington, we gave him the names of several hotels in the area around the Hilton where we thought he might have stayed, but he still couldn't remember where he had spent the previous night. He did say, however, that his room key was among the possessions that had been taken from him in the cellblock downstairs.

It turned out that he had stayed at the Park Central, an older, moderately priced hotel that has since been torn down. Located at the corner of Eighteenth and G streets, it was just two blocks from the White House and almost across the street from Secret Service headquarters.

During the time I was with Hinckley, he didn't speak very often. I was talking with other federal and city police officers who were coming in and out of the interview room, but I was trying to avoid any conversations about the shooting in front of Hinckley since discussing it could possibly damage the government's case against him. At this point, I still didn't know who, if anyone, had been hit by the gunfire at the Hilton. I didn't want to ask anyone in front of Hinckley, but, since he remained officially in my custody, I wasn't going to leave the room to ask about the shooting. It would be more than three hours after the shooting before I found out that, in addition to President Reagan, White House Press Secretary James S. Brady had been critically injured and that two fellow law-enforcement officers, Secret Service Agent Timothy McCarthy and Officer Thomas K. Delahanty of the Washington police, had also been wounded.

I thought at the time it was strange that all during this period the man who had just shot at the President never once mentioned the incident or asked if he had hit anyone. Perhaps Hinckley was already thinking of his legal defense, but he didn't seem interested in finding out whom he had shot or if anyone had been killed. He was a picture of calm. He never shook or stammered as I have watched many criminals do when they were first brought into a police station after being arrested.

A federal court jury later would find Hinckley not guilty by reason of insanity, and order him committed to St. Elizabeth's Hospital in Washington.

I must say, however, that never during the three hours that Hinckley was in my custody immediately following the shooting did I get the impression that he was mentally ill. Of course, I have no formal psychological training, but during my Secret Service career I interviewed literally hundreds of mentally disturbed people, and I don't put John W. Hinckley, Jr., in that category. Despite my lack of formal training, my ability to judge people's mental stability has been proven many times.

As a senior agent at the White House for more than two years, I was called to the gate numerous times by the guards to interview people who were trying to get in. Of the approximately two dozen people I had sent from the gate of the White House to St. Elizabeth's for observation, the hospital staff admitted all but one or two of them. Had Hinckley appeared in front of the White House acting as he did in the interview room at Washington police headquarters, I wouldn't have thought of calling St. Elizabeth's.

He sat there calmly, occasionally rubbing his wrist, and while he sometimes appeared to be in deep thought, he had no trouble whatsoever following what was going on around him. He didn't mention Jodie Foster, the young actress he later claimed he was trying to impress by shooting the President, although FBI agents searching his hotel room later that evening found a letter he had written to her.

I think that I, having waited for over sixteen years to react to such an incident, was more nervous than Hinckley. I was like a spring coiled for years, waiting to be released. Most Secret Service agents go through their entire careers without ever finding out how they would react in such a situation. After Jerry Parr, Ray Shaddick, Tim McCarthy, and I were awarded Medals of Valor, the Secret Service's highest award, for our actions during the shooting, H. Stuart Knight, then director of the service, said, "What sets these men apart from the fifteen hundred and sixty other special agents is that they were at that place at that time."

I agree with him. The Secret Service is a very professional organization and the training to react the way the four of us did outside the Hilton is constant. But I also believe that within everyone there is something—an instinct, a natural tendency toward self-preservation, or whatever—that makes each of us look out for our own self-interest, even if we might later consider ourselves cowards. I have always thought of this as the sleeping dragon within all of us.

Although I would go through a period of severe mental stress following the shooting, and my second marriage would break up, I had met my dragon on that gray spring afternoon, and I had conquered him.

CHAPTER 4

The Service Reacts

Hinckley's shots at the Hilton set off a chain of events for the Secret Service and other federal agencies that stretched from a pawn shop in Dallas to the money markets of Hong Kong and Singapore. As my partner and I were racing toward D.C. police headquarters with the suspect, word of the shooting was being relayed to various Secret Service divisions and other federal law-enforcement personnel through official communications channels. Within minutes, the public heard about the incident on radio and television and, in fact, that is also how most government officials learned that shots had been fired at the President.

Following routine procedures for such events, security planning for the visit to the Hilton had begun the previous Wednesday, March 25, when Bill Green was designated the lead advance agent by the Presidential Protective Division of the Secret Service. Green was responsible for coordinating all security preparations. The White House staff advance man, Rick Ahearn, was responsible for the President's schedule during the visit.

On Friday morning, March 27, Green, Ahearn, and members of their respective advance teams met with Hilton representatives and officials of the Building and Construction Trades Union to make arrangements for the speech to that group. By Friday evening, all agents on the Secret Service advance team had been notified of their assignments for the following Monday. Over the weekend, Green and Agent Mary Ann Gordon, who was in charge of transportation for the event, arranged for the participation of other Secret Service agents and police officers who would be needed to provide security while the President was out of the White House.

On Monday morning, Gordon checked with the city highway department to make sure no construction was scheduled that day along the motorcade route. Later, she drove the route with a representative of the police department. When the President left the White House at 1:45 P.M. for the five-minute trip up Connecticut Avenue, everyone involved knew what his or her job was. Most of the participants had made the same trip under similar circumstances many times before. The Metropolitan Police Department and United States Park Police who assist the service with presidential trips in Washington are familiar with Secret Service procedures and are able to provide drivers, motorcycle escorts, and crowd control with relatively little briefing or advance preparation. When the President arrived at the Washington Hilton's VIP entrance at 1:50 P.M., the ballroom where he was to speak had been swept for bombs by the service's Technical Security Division, explosive-ordnance disposal personnel and a countersniper team were on duty, and nothing appeared amiss. As far as the Secret Service was concerned, the Hilton visit was uncomplicated.

The only problem thus far had been a minor one. A Park Police officer had forgotten to bring a portable two-way radio for use in one of the leading motorcade cars, so agents in the motorcade had no communications with escorting Park Police motorcycle officers. On the way to the hotel, Ray Shaddick, shift leader on the White House detail, called Green for a situation report. Green noted that there were about seven press people and about ten spectators at the rope line thirty-five to forty feet from the entrance, but that he was aware of no problems and the arrival area was clear. When his limousine arrived at the entrance, the President waited until the agents with him were in position around the car. Then he got out, was met by Ahearn at the door, and went inside the hotel.

While Reagan addressed the crowd inside, the vehicles in the motorcade were turned around to face a gap in the concrete island dividing the hotel's driveway from T Street. This was standard procedure for a Hilton visit, and it brought the presidential limousine to within fifteen to twenty feet of the rope line, requiring the President to walk about thirty feet from the door of the hotel back to his car.

I have been asked many times why Hinckley was allowed to get so close to the President that day and why he was permitted in a press area. My answer has always been that it wasn't a designated press area. Every journalist and electronic-media technician who covers the White House is issued a special pass by the Secret Service. This laminated identification card, with a color photo of the person to whom it is issued, is similar to the ID card carried by members of the White House staff and agents themselves. In order to enter a designated press area, a reporter or technician must wear it in plain sight. Without one, Hinckley would never have been allowed in a press area. Since it's not up to the Secret Service but up to the White House staff to decide what is and is not a press area, I can only defend the Secret Service in this case. Anyone in the world could have walked up to that rope line and the agents there would have had no reason to issue a challenge unless that person acted suspiciously or made a threatening move toward the President.

At 2:20 P.M., Bill Green radioed from inside the ballroom that

Reagan was finishing his speech and would be departing shortly. All of the motorcade drivers returned to their vehicles and the security car that was to precede the motorcade back to the White House by a few minutes left.

President Reagan walked through the doorway at 2:27 P.M., accompanied by members of the White House Secret Service detail and several White House staffers, including Press Secretary James Brady, Deputy Chief of Staff Michael Deaver, and military aide José Muratti. Detail leader Jerry Parr and shift leader Ray Shaddick were directly behind the President. The first shot was fired when Reagan was just three feet from the limousine door that Agent Tim McCarthy was holding open. Immediately, Tim turned in the direction of the shots, spread his arms and legs to protect the President, and took a bullet in the abdomen.

His action was precisely what it should have been. All agents are taught that if shots are fired they should remain in an upright position and make themselves as large a target as possible. This procedure is practiced regularly at the service's training facility in Beltsville, Maryland, a Washington suburb. Exercises there are designed to condition agents' responses to an attack on the person whom they are protecting. In the classroom, in practical training, and on the job, agents are taught that the safety of the protected person is their primary concern. They are trained to put themselves between the President and the source of the shots. They are to see to his safety and evacuation before attempting to subdue an assailant or even to prevent an assailant's escape.

After Shaddick helped push the President and Parr into the limousine, he slammed the door and then jumped into the follow-up car as the motorcade sped away.

"We've had shots fired, shots fired, there are some injuries" Shaddick radioed the Presidential Protective Division's command post in the White House.

No Secret Service agent or other law-enforcement officer at the scene had seen Hinckley draw the .22 caliber pistol he used to shoot the President and three others. Several agents and Washington police officers ran to the rope line after the shots had been fired to assist me in subduing Hinckley. Other agents, reacting according to training, attempted to determine if there were any other assailants in the crowd across T Street and protected the motorcade's departure.

Agent Bob Wanko, a member of the White House detail, drew an Israeli-made Uzi submachine gun to protect the rear of the motorcade as it left the scene. Several other agents and police officers also drew weapons, but no shots were fired by law-enforcement personnel and the only people hurt were the ones hit by Hinckley's bullets.

There was some momentary confusion when a Park Police motorcycle officer, rushing to assist in subduing Hinckley, dropped his service revolver near the spot where White House Press Secretary Jim Brady lay critically wounded. At first, some other officers and spectators thought the park policeman's pistol was the one used in the shooting, but Agent Thomas Lightsey had already used his handcuffs to pick up Hinckley's gun from the sidewalk where it had fallen when I tackled Hinckley.

About ten seconds after the first shot, the President's limousine pulled away from the curb and turned onto T Street. It passed another motorcade car that had stalled going up a hill, along with some of the police motorcycles that remained parked, and turned left onto Connecticut Avenue. Mary Ann Gordon had left her car and run toward the presidential limousine when the shots were fired. Seeing that the President was already in the limousine, however, she jumped into another motorcade car, waited momentarily for the President's personal physician, who always travels with him, and then ordered the driver to pull in behind the limousine. Because of the confusion and the crowd around the other vehicles, the main follow-up car was unable to leave the scene until thirteen seconds after the President's car had departed.

The first radio transmission after the limousine departed was from Parr to Shaddick. "[The President]* is okay, follow-up. [The President] is okay," Parr said.

"You want to go to the hospital or back to the White House?" Shaddick asked.

"We're going right, we're going to [the White House]."

Seconds later, however, President Reagan told Parr he was having trouble breathing and Parr saw blood in his mouth. That was when Parr told agent Drew Unrue, who was driving, to go to the hospital instead.

"We want to go to the emergency room of George Washington," Unrue radioed Gordon.

After Gordon acknowledged the transmission, Unrue added, "Go to George Washington *fast.*"

Parr then radioed Shaddick that they were going to the hospital emergency room and added, "Get an ambulance—I mean get—ah—stretcher out there."

Parr later said that he hadn't broadcast that the President was hurt because he hadn't wanted everyone who was monitoring the Secret Service radio frequency to know of Reagan's injury.

Shaddick then asked the command post at the White House if it had copied Parr's last transmission that the motorcade was going to George Washington University Hospital. The command post replied that it had and that a call had already been made to the hospital.

The command post told the hospital that the President was en route and that there were injuries, but didn't say that the President was injured or that a stretcher should be available.

When Gordon attempted to notify the police escort that the motorcade was going to the hospital, she was unable to do so because of the heavy radio traffic on the police frequency. In order

---

* Parr used the Secret Service code words for President Reagan and the White House. Code names are assigned to all officials the service protects and to locations that they frequently visit. While not officially classified, the names are kept as confidential as possible and I won't reveal them here.

to keep a car in front of the President's, she ordered her driver to pass the limousine. When the motorcade turned onto Pennsylvania Avenue from Seventeenth Street, the leading police car and four motorcycles failed to make the turn, continuing instead to the White House. Gordon's car led the limousine to the hospital.

After the call from the White House command post, one of the hospital emergency-room personnel announced over a loudspeaker that the President was coming in. Fred White, assistant director of the Secret Service for administration, happened to be in the emergency room at the time on a personal matter. Hearing the announcement, he ordered the emergency-room doors held open and went outside to meet the limousine, which arrived at 2:30 P.M.—three minutes after the shooting.

President Reagan got out of the car and started to walk into the emergency room. Inside the hospital, Reagan's knees began to buckle and he was carried the rest of the way to Trauma Bay 5 by Parr, Shaddick, and two paramedics. At this point, he appeared to be in the initial stages of shock.

Medical personnel immediately started to administer the standard emergency treatment. The President's clothes were removed, he was placed on oxygen and an intravenous solution, and a blood sample taken to determine his blood type. However, Parr knew that Reagan's blood type was O-positive, thereby saving crucial minutes in beginning the treatment.

It wasn't until after the President's clothes had been removed that the medical staff realized he had been shot. A tube was inserted into his chest and thirteen hundred cubic centimeters of blood were removed from his left lung. Within ten minutes of his arrival at the hospital, he began receiving transfusions of universal donor blood. Although Reagan remained conscious and talked with members of the medical staff and with Mrs. Reagan when she arrived, his condition was much more serious than was first reported.

Doctors later said that the President lost about half of the total volume of blood in his body before he went into surgery. Had the incident not occurred within a three-minute drive of a first-class, fully equipped trauma center like the one at George Washington University Hospital, the President could have died from shock or loss of blood.

Two of the recommendations following the shooting were that a trained paramedic team always travel with the President and that a copy of his medical records be carried in the limousine. In this case, the paramedic team would have made little difference due to the closeness of the hospital, but the President's medical records were neither at the hospital nor with the motorcade. Although Parr knew his correct blood type, a medical history could possibly have saved a few minutes in beginning the treatment.

As the medical team began treating the gunshot wound to Reagan's chest, the Secret Service agents present quickly had to establish a security net around the hospital. That duty fell mainly to Shaddick, since it was Parr's responsibility to remain with the President.

When the motorcade had arrived, Shaddick instructed Agent Dennis Fabel, driver of the follow-up car, to radio the White House command post for more manpower. The hospital administrator had already activated the hospital's disaster plan, which limited public access to the building somewhat, and with the assistance of hospital personnel, the agents who had accompanied the President began to establish checkpoints at the entrance to the emergency room, excluding everyone except those identified as necessary medical personnel.

Mary Ann Gordon remained outside the emergency-room entrance and began setting up security around the hospital. As members of the news media and the public began to gather, she asked the Washington and Park Police officers present for assistance in establishing crowd control. By 3:30 most of the city and park policemen had been replaced by officers from the Secret Service Uniformed Division.

A few minutes after the President entered the emergency room, the four-to-midnight-shift agents arrived at the hospital. They had been driving to work at the time of the shooting and were ordered to report directly to the hospital. Shaddick assigned them to assist in securing the emergency room, locating a command post, establishing communications, and preparing for the President's expected move to the operating room, recovery room, and intensive care unit.

Within an hour after the shooting, Pat Miller, assistant to the special agent in charge of the Washington field office, arrived, along with agents from the Technical Security Division and personnel from the White House Communications Agency.

By the time the President was out of surgery at about 5:45 P.M., the basic security plan that would remain in place for the duration of his stay in the hospital was functioning. A command post and communications center had been established in Room 2500, canine and countersniper teams were in place, and personnel from the Uniformed Division were guarding the entrances to the hospital, which, for the next few weeks, would almost be an annex to the White House as far as security was concerned.

Vice-President George Bush was aboard Air Force Two en route from Fort Worth to Austin, Texas, when he was notified of the shooting. He decided to land in Austin, refuel, and return to Washington. The Vice-President didn't leave his plane during the 45-minute refueling stop, and agents on board guarded the doors with automatic weapons while the plane was on the ground.

Two agents who were at Andrews Air Force Base, just outside Washington, for the arrival of the Prime Minister of the Netherlands were ordered to remain there pending Bush's arrival. Several other agents were sent to Andrews also. When the Vice-President landed at 6:25 P.M., his plane taxied directly into a hangcr adjaccnt to thc onc housing Air Force One and Bush was flown by helicopter to the Vice-President's residence on the grounds of the Naval Observatory, landing there at 6:41 P.M. From there, he transferred to an armored limousine and was escorted by an augmented motorcade to the White House, where he remained until nearly 10 P.M.

White House Chief of Staff James Baker and Presidential Counselor Ed Meese were informed of the shooting within minutes and went from the White House to the hospital.

Although no formal national emergency was declared, Secretary of State Alexander M. Haig, Jr., Defense Secretary Caspar W. Weinberger, Attorney General William French Smith, Treasury Secretary Donald Regan, CIA Director William Casey, and National Security Adviser Richard Allen all reported to the situation room in the basement of the White House West Wing, where they remained until it was clear that the President was out of immediate medical danger.

About fifteen minutes after the shooting, the Bureau of Alcohol, Tobacco, and Firearms ordered its National Firearms Tracing Center to stand by for an urgent trace. At 3:20 P.M. the Secret Service contacted ATF with a description and serial number of the weapon recovered from the scene of the assassination attempt. A few minutes later, ATF called back to say that one digit was missing from the serial number. The number of digits varies according to the manufacturer, so it was immediately apparent to ATF personnel that a number had been dropped. About 4 P.M., the service corrected its mistake and provided ATF with the right number. A trace began immediately.

The chief of the National Firearms Tracing Center phoned the manufacturer, RG Industries in Miami, and was advised in a few minutes that the weapon had been shipped on July 27, 1979, to Scott Wholesale in Indian Trail, North Carolina. A call to that company revealed that the gun had been sold to Rocky's Pawn Shop at 2018 Elm Street, Dallas, on October 11, 1979. The chief then called the pawn shop where the files showed that the gun had been purchased on October 13, 1980, by a man identifying himself as John Warnock Hinckley, Jr. For identification he had provided his Texas driver's license number, his date of birth, and an address in Lubbock, Texas. The pawn shop also told ATF that Hinckley had purchased a second identical gun on the same day.

By 4:55 P.M. agents from the ATF, Secret Service, and FBI Dallas field offices were on their way to Rocky's to obtain the originals of Form 4473 that Hinckley had signed when he purchased the two RG Industries .22 caliber revolvers.

While ATF headquarters was conducting the gun trace from Washington, agents in the ATF Lubbock field office, after learning from television reports that the suspect was from the Lubbock area, began calling gun dealers in the city and asking them to check their records for purchases by Hinckley.

The Lubbock office found that Hinckley had made several other purchases of firearms and ammunition, including a box of explosive bullets sold under the brand name Devastator. ATF headquarters received this information at about 6 P.M. and immediately passed it on to the chief of ATF's Firearms Technology Branch, who began a search of his files for information on the bullets. President Reagan was already out of surgery by the time it was known that the bullets Hinckley had used might possibly contain small explosive charges, and the information was never passed on to the medical personnel treating the other three men wounded in the incident. This was an obvious oversight that could have had tragic results, but as it turned out, Hinckley hadn't used the explosive ammunition and there was no danger to people in the operating rooms.

About 6:30 P.M., the FBI asked ATF for a trace on the three pistols that had been confiscated from Hinckley when he was arrested at the Nashville airport in 1980. These weapons turned out to be the ones Hinckley had bought in Lubbock.

While ATF was able to provide information on the weapon used to shoot Reagan within an hour after receiving the correct

serial number, such a rapid response wouldn't have been possible
had the shooting not occurred during normal business hours.
Federal law requires dealers to keep records on all firearms sold,
and in this case all the dealers, from manufacturer to retailer, had
the proper forms. Had it been the middle of the night, however,
it would have been difficult to contact the offices where the forms
were located, and ATF's tracing center doesn't normally operate
except during regular business hours.

Treasury Secretary Regan's Secret Service detail notified him
of the attempted assassination within minutes after the shooting,
and the Secretary immediately left his office for the White
House. Meanwhile, key Treasury Department and Federal Reserve Board officials began keeping a close watch on the national
and world financial markets and preparing to intervene, if necessary, to support the value of the American dollar.

At the time of the shooting, the key Treasury domestic-finance
officials—Undersecretary for Monetary Affairs–Designate Beryl
Sprinkel, Assistant Secretary–Designate Roger W. Mehle, Jr.,
and Acting Assistant Secretary John E. Schmidt—were all attending a meeting in Sprinkel's office. (At the time, the three
held "designate" or "acting" titles because Reagan had been in
office for just over two months and their appointments hadn't yet
been confirmed by Congress.) The Secretary's office called Sprinkel with news of the shooting at about 2:40 P.M., and the meeting
was immediately adjourned. Mehle and Schmidt went to the
Treasury market room outside Schmidt's office to watch the reaction of the financial markets.

When initial news reports indicated that the President hadn't
been hit, the stock market reaction wasn't particularly sharp. The
Dow-Jones Industrial Average fell from 998 at 2:30 P.M. to 992 at
3 P.M. But selling pressure was building. When word came that
the President had, in fact, been shot, Schmidt returned to the
market room and called Douglas Scarff, director of market regula-
tion at the Securities and Exchange Commission. Scarff told him

that all the financial markets had already closed voluntarily without waiting for an order from Washington.

At the first reports of the shooting, the governors of the various exchanges had acted quickly to prepare for a rapid shutdown. New York Stock Exchange officials had been observing the buildup in selling pressure, and when the wire services reported at 3:16 P.M. that the President had been wounded, trading was stopped within one minute. All other U.S. financial markets closed within six minutes. This action prevented a repetition of the sharp decline that had followed the assassination of President Kennedy in 1963 (when the Dow-Jones Industrial Average fell twenty-one points in less than thirty minutes with an estimated loss of eleven billion dollars) and President Eisenhower's heart attack in 1955, when the estimated paper loss was fourteen billion.

At the time of the shooting, the Federal Reserve Bank of New York was in the process of executing an order for five hundred million dollars in Treasury bills for a foreign customer. Since initial news reports indicated that the President hadn't been hit, Federal Reserve officials decided to execute the order routinely— in part to signal stability and calm to the world money markets. Before the transaction was completed, word came that the President had been wounded, but the order was still executed as usual. Otherwise, trading stopped.

Under the Gold Reserve Act of 1934, the Secretary of the Treasury is authorized to utilize the Exchange Stabilization Fund to deal in gold and foreign currency as he may deem necessary for "orderly exchange arrangements and a stable system of exchange rates." On April 27, 1978, the United States notified the International Monetary Fund that its "authorities [will] intervene when necessary to counter disorderly conditions in the exchange markets." In layman's language that means that the United States will act to protect the value of the dollar when necessary. This isn't done very often, but the Treasury Department and Federal

Reserve Board moved quickly to use their authority on March 30, 1981.

Authority over the Exchange Stabilization Fund is delegated to the director of the Treasury Department's Office of Foreign Exchange Operations, who at the time of the shooting was Frederick L. Springborn.

Coincidentally, the attempt on President Reagan's life took place within three minutes of the daily 2:30 P.M. conference call among Springborn, Ted Truman (director of the Federal Reserve Board's International Division), and the personnel on duty at the New York Federal Reserve Bank's foreign trading desk. The New York Fed's domestic trading desk, which routinely monitors all news wires, passed word of the shooting to the foreign desk during the conference call.

Measured against West German currency, the dollar had opened in New York at 2.1243 marks on March 30, 1981, and had declined to 2.0755 marks by 2:30 P.M. Eastern Standard Time. In other words, that morning $1 would buy 2.1243 marks, but by 2:30 it would buy only 2.0755 marks. While this may seem like a very slight difference, those hundredths of a point translate into millions of dollars for American corporations doing business overseas.

Immediately after broadcast reports of the shooting, the dollar dropped to 2.0650 marks on virtually no trading. At 2:43 P.M., Reuters, the British worldwide news agency, carried a story on its wire stating that President Reagan hadn't been hit. Reuters is particularly influential at such times since it is a major source of news in Europe, the Middle East, and the Far East and has a reputation for more than a century of accurate, unbiased reporting. Shortly after the Reuters story, the dollar rose slightly, back up to 2.0675 marks.

Between 2:45 and 3 P.M., news reports of what had happened at the Washington Hilton remained unclear and conflicting, but pressure on the dollar began to build in the exchange markets as belief grew that the President had been shot.

Trading wasn't very active and the dollar remained at around 2.0650 marks, but Treasury Department officials watching the market decided that official U.S. government intervention would be helpful to steady market conditions and prevent speculative selling of dollars. Springborn conferred with Thomas B. C. Leddy, deputy assistant secretary for international monetary affairs, who then went to Sprinkel's office. All three men concurred that intervention should be authorized.

Meanwhile, Federal Reserve Board officials had been actively watching the exchange markets from the Fed's office a few blocks west of the White House, on Constitution Avenue. The Federal Reserve Board has authority to intervene in foreign exchange operations through its System Open Market Account, run by its New York bank. The manager of the New York Federal Reserve Bank's foreign department happened to be visiting the Federal Reserve Board office in Washington at the time of the shooting. He was thus able to confer on the spot with senior Federal Reserve officials who were monitoring the situation.

At 3:30 P.M., fourteen minutes after the Associated Press and United Press International reported that President Reagan had been wounded, the New York Fed began selling West German marks and buying U.S. dollars through several New York brokers. This approach was used so word would spread quickly through the dealers to their major clients that the U.S. government was buying dollars while at the same time making it impossible for anyone to determine the extent of the intervention.

The market intervention continued until 5 P.M., when trading effectively stopped for the day in New York. In an hour and a half, the equivalent of $74.4 million in West German marks had been sold by the New York Federal Reserve Bank and the dollar had been supported at about 2.0650 marks.

The New York trading desk remained in operation throughout the night of March 30–31, ready to intervene in the Hong Kong and Singapore markets if necessary. But no further action was required because the dollar rose to 2.0735 marks in early Hong

Kong trading and to 2.0973 marks when the Frankfurt market opened at about 2 A.M. Eastern Standard Time. Treasury Department analysts later attributed this favorable trend to a combination of the promising medical reports on President Reagan's condition issued by George Washington University Hospital and the knowledge throughout the world financial markets that the United States had acted quickly to support the dollar.

All of this activity took place after the shooting. What is harder to assess is whether anything more could have been done to prevent it. All of the investigations that took place in the spring and summer of 1981 by congressional committees and executive branch departments concluded that those of us who were at the Hilton that day did everything humanly possible to stop Hinckley and get the President out of harm's way. But there are, of course, the "ifs."

If I had gotten to Hinckley one second sooner, the force of my body hitting his would probably have deflected the shot that hit the President. Someone else, quite possibly myself, might have been hit, but the President wouldn't have been shot.

If Tim McCarthy had moved two or three feet to his right, he might have been hit by the bullet that struck Reagan instead of by one of Hinckley's other shots.

If Jerry Parr's reflexes had been a split second faster or slower, he wouldn't have been pushing the President into the limousine at the exact instant the bullet glanced off the car and hit Reagan.

None of these things really matter, however. All the Secret Service agents present that day reacted as fast as they could and exactly as they all had been trained to behave in such a situation. The real question is: Should the Secret Service have known about Hinckley before he got close enough to the President to fire his pistol? The fact that we didn't know about Hinckley's mental condition—and the reason that the Secret Service still doesn't have records on possibly hundreds or even thousands of other people who are potential threats to the President—is a matter of national policy over which the service has almost no control.

Physically surrounding the President isn't sufficient protection. His ultimate shield must be the ability of the Secret Service to keep him out of dangerous environments. The service will never be able to do this without adequate intelligence information on the intentions and plans of potentially dangerous people.

Since 1976, when a new set of domestic security guidelines was issued by then Attorney General Edward Levi, the amount of information reaching the service from other law-enforcement agencies has vastly declined. The guidelines prevent the FBI from engaging in domestic intelligence gathering unless it is in possession of "specific and articulable facts giving reason to believe that an individual or a group is or may be engaged in activities which involve the use of force or violence and which involve or will involve the violation of federal law. . . ."

A Treasury Department report following the assassination attempt concluded that "one of the lessons of March 30 is that the President is exposed to danger whenever he is outside the White House and the best efforts of alert agents on the scene cannot substitute for adequate warning."

How drastically the potential for "adequate warning" declined after 1976 was illustrated by a General Accounting Office report issued in November 1977. The GAO, which works for Congress rather than for the executive branch of the government, found that as of June 30, 1977, the FBI had a total of 642 domestic intelligence matters pending, compared to 9,814 on the same date in 1975, before the new guidelines went into effect. The same GAO study found that in June 1975, there were 1,454 domestic intelligence cases opened by the FBI. Two years later, in June 1977, the number had dropped to 95.

Intelligence information can be divided into two broad categories: information about the intentions and objectives of individuals and groups, and information about actions that individuals or groups have already taken. The Secret Service is interested primarily in the first category, data that will enable it to predict possible threats to the President. Following the issuance of the

Attorney General's guidelines, however, the FBI began to place almost all of its intelligence-gathering emphasis on the second category, incidents that already had taken place, in order to build strong criminal cases for U.S. attorneys to prosecute.

In November 1979, then Secret Service Director Knight told the Senate Judiciary Committee that the service was receiving only about 40 percent of the information it had previously received from the FBI and that even this reduced intelligence product had deteriorated in quality. Explaining what he meant by quality, Knight cited the loss of information concerning the motives and plans of groups or individuals that might pose a threat to the President. Knight repeated these statements in testimony before other congressional committees following the shooting, specifically attributing the loss of useful intelligence to the Attorney General's Domestic Security Guidelines. As I said earlier, the guidelines are a matter of national policy. They were instituted by the Ford administration and continued through the Carter and Reagan administrations. Three presidents and five elected Congresses have apparently felt they are in the best interest of the country, but that doesn't mean that they don't make it harder for the Secret Service to do its job.

Even when the service has sufficient intelligence, however, classifying someone as "dangerous to the President" is, at best, a very subjective judgment. During the 1960s and 1970s, several outside studies were commissioned by Secret Service headquarters to try to develop a profile of the type of individual likely to be dangerous to the President. But as a Treasury Department report following the Hinckley shooting noted, "These efforts produced little useful information." So in the absence of any reliable statistical data, the determination of who is dangerous and who isn't is based almost entirely on the judgment of individual Secret Service agents.

A person who has been determined to be a threat to the President, or someone else under Secret Service protection, is interviewed by agents at regular intervals and his or her whereabouts are periodically monitored. This continues until the field office in charge of the investigation decides that the person being monitored no longer presents a danger to a high government official and the service's Intelligence Division concurs in that judgment. At the time of the attempt on President Reagan's life, there were about four hundred people on the "dangerous" list, but many of them were in mental institutions or prisons. Hinckley wasn't among them.

The service's Foreign Intelligence Branch also keeps files on international terrorist groups that might be a threat to a protected person. Certain groups that are considered the most dangerous are constantly monitored, while others are reviewed only occasionally. As in the case of individuals, there is no "dangerous group" profile and assessments are based on agent judgment and on analysis done by the Intelligence Division and other law-enforcement or national security agencies.

Here again, however, decisions made as a matter of national policy have made it more difficult for the Secret Service to do its job. Former Director Knight told Congress on several different occasions that the Freedom of Information Act and the Privacy Act had both contributed to a decrease in the intelligence information received by the Secret Service from several sources, including other law-enforcement agencies and foreign governments.

Under the Freedom of Information Act, any individual or group, including the news media, can obtain many government records that were previously confidential. The Privacy Act often makes it difficult for government agencies to share information with each other, especially when the information must pass between a federal agency and its state or local counterpart.

In testimony before committees of both the House of Representatives and the Senate following the Reagan assassination attempt, Knight noted that foreign law-enforcement organizations, as well as state and local police departments, are reluctant to share information with the Secret Service and other federal agencies. This reluctance, Knight suggested, is largely the result of the Freedom of Information Act and the Privacy Act, which have led foreign and other information sources to believe that United States government law-enforcement agencies cannot maintain the confidentiality of the information they receive. This view is almost universally shared by other federal law-enforcement officials.

In a 1978 report to Congress, the U.S. comptroller general noted that "law enforcement officials at all levels of government have stated in Congressional testimony that the proliferation of access and privacy laws has been instrumental in creating a restrictive climate which affects their ability to obtain information from the public and institutions, to recruit and maintain informants, and to exchange information with other law enforcement agencies."

Senior Secret Service officials have told Congress that, since most of the threats against the President's life come from mentally unstable people, timely access to records maintained by mental institutions is critical when the President or other dignitaries under Secret Service protection travel around the country. Unfortunately, according to the GAO report, many law-enforcement officials have reported that the Privacy Act has severe effects on their ability to obtain information from institutions such as hospitals, banks, and telephone companies. While law-enforcement officers could previously obtain records from these institutions on an informal basis, an increasing number of them require that agents obtain a subpoena before they will provide the information.

It has been seven years since the comptroller general outlined these problems in detail for Congress, but nothing has changed. It is just as difficult now for the Secret Service to obtain background information quickly on someone who threatens the President as it was when the report was first presented to Congress in

1978, and coordinating the information that *is* available is sometimes as difficult as obtaining it in the first place.

An example of the difficulties involved is the arrest of Hinckley at the Nashville airport on October 9, 1980— nearly six months before he shot President Reagan. As I said earlier, Hinckley was arrested when he attempted to board a commercial airliner while carrying three pistols. President Carter was speaking less than ten miles away at the time. Even though he could have legally checked them through to his destination in his baggage, Hinckley attempted to carry the weapons into the passenger cabin and was arrested by airport police when they were detected. This raised questions from Congress and the news media following the Reagan assassination attempt about whether the Secret Service should have known that Hinckley posed a threat to the President.

The Nashville arrest coincided with a substantial amount of presidential campaign activity in Tennessee. Not only was President Carter conducting a "town meeting" at the Grand Ole Opry that day, but Joan Mondale, the Vice-President's wife, also had been campaigning in Nashville the day before. Ronald Reagan, then the Republican nominee for President, had just canceled a trip to Memphis scheduled for October 8.

Local police considered the arrest routine and unrelated to Carter's visit, a reasonable assumption considering that the President was still speaking when Hinckley was arrested for trying to board a plane that would have taken him miles away from Nashville by the time Carter returned to the airport.

The arrest was reported by Nashville authorities to the FBI, nevertheless, because attempting to board an aircraft with weapons is a violation of federal as well as local law. The FBI didn't refer the case to the United States attorney for middle Tennessee, however, assuming that he would automatically decline to prosecute the case. Neither did the FBI pass the information along to the Secret Service; this decision was not unreasonable in light of the hundreds of such arrests annually in the United States and in that nothing in the circumstances suggested that Hinckley was or would become a threat to the President.

There is an agreement between the FBI and the Secret Service to share information relevant to each other's jurisdictions, but this agreement in no way requires the FBI to send every arrest report it receives from local police departments to the service. If that happened, the Secret Service Intelligence Division would be buried in an avalanche of paper. And as the Treasury Department follow-up report on the assassination attempt noted, "Even assuming that the information had been passed on to the Service by the FBI, one cannot conclude that the consequences would have been different."

The Secret Service doesn't have nearly enough agents to interview everyone who is arrested for relatively minor crimes in each city the President visits in the course of a political campaign. The most the service could have done with the information on the Hinckley arrest would have been to store it for later correlation with other facts about him. If, for example, he had been arrested in another city that the President was visiting, the coincidence might have suggested that he was stalking the President and led to a more thorough investigation. But Hinckley wasn't arrested again before he shot President Reagan, and even if he had been, the Secret Service's manpower and resources for correlating such information are limited at best.

CHAPTER 5

The Aftermath

As the afternoon wore on at Washington police headquarters following the shooting and the tension subsided somewhat, my neck and back began to hurt. I mentioned this to one of the officers in the interview room where we were still holding Hinckley, remarking that I had been at the bottom of a pile of agents and police officers at the hotel.

Hinckley quickly looked up and corrected me. I hadn't been at the bottom of the pile, he said, he had. It was almost as if he wanted to join us in a friendly conversation.

The guy has most of his marbles, I remember thinking.

Two officers from the police department's crime lab came into the interview room and advised Hinckley that District of Columbia law required them to run a test on his hands to determine if there was any residue of powder on them from firing a gun. He was cooperative and sat there, saying nothing, as they went over his hands and fingers with cotton swabs.

There was one time Hinckley could possibly have washed his

hands, and I was trying to remember if he had. He had been standing by a sink in the cell downstairs right after we brought him in, but I couldn't remember his turning on the water. My mind had been very busy at the time with trying to remember to do everything by the book so I wouldn't violate any of his rights. I had also been concerned that he might try to hurt himself.

Although the test wasn't really necessary with all the other evidence against him, it turned out that he hadn't washed his hands, and the results were positive.

From time to time, a Secret Service agent, FBI agent, or Washington police officer would come to the door of the room where we still had Hinckley handcuffed to an interview table and say something to one of us inside. Hinckley always appeared alert, looking up to see who was at the door. But he still didn't ask anything about the shooting. I was curious about what had happened, and especially about whether the President had been shot, but I managed to refrain from asking any questions in front of Hinckley.

About five o'clock, an FBI agent came in to tell me that I was relieved of my watch over Hinckley since the FBI had taken custody of him from the Secret Service. I asked the agent to see if there were any Secret Service supervisors in the outer office and, if so, to please ask one of them to come to the interview room. Ed Dansereau, my immediate supervisor in the Washington field office, soon appeared at the door. I told him what the FBI agent had said, adding that I felt it was necessary to be relieved by one of my own supervisors.

Before I walked out of the room, I took one last, long look at Hinckley. There still was no expression on his face. We exchanged glances, but no words.

When I walked into the big squad room of the Metropolitan Police Department's homicide section, it was full of federal and city officers. Everyone was extremely busy. The pent-up tension of three hours began to drain away. My first thought after I left

Hinckley was *I only have three years left in the service before I retire. I really don't need this now.*

There would be more than the usual amount of pressure during the next weeks and months. The shooting would be investigated over and over and so would the Secret Service. All of our procedures would be examined in detail, as would the actions of everyone present when the shooting took place. There would be a criminal case to prepare against Hinckley. And I would be right in the middle of it all.

I was already under a great deal of stress from problems at home. I had been married to my second wife, Helenmae (whom I called H.M.), for two and a half years at the time of the shooting. She was a flight attendant for a major airline and away from home as much as I was. I was certain that at least one other man was interested in her. We had been seeing a counselor for several months, but our marriage was on the verge of breaking up. As I stood there in the squad room, I felt it was tough enough to handle one major crisis in my life; I didn't need a second one. For a moment, I almost broke down right there, but I forced myself to think about other things.

A television set in the squad room was carrying the news that Reagan had been shot and was undergoing surgery at George Washington University Hospital. I found another agent to brief me, so I could finally find out what had happened. I have since thought about how ironic it was that I was probably one of the last people in the country to learn what had occurred outside the Washington Hilton nearly three hours earlier. But even after finding out that Hinckley had wounded four people, I still didn't feel any hatred toward him. Maybe I would have felt differently if someone had been killed, but at that moment, I was simply relieved to know that no one was dead.

About 5:30, Ed Dansereau came over and told me that since I was the senior agent at the police station, he was going to assign me as the case agent. I looked at him in disbelief. It was inconceivable to me that he wanted me to handle the sheaf of detailed paperwork that had to be started immediately and would take most of the night. I was barely capable of holding a complete thought in my head.

"Ed, you can't be serious," I said. "You'd be wise to select someone who wasn't involved in the shooting." I guess he saw my point, since he assigned another agent to the case.

As I relaxed a little more, my neck and back really began to hurt. I was beginning to think that my neck might have been seriously injured in the pileup at the hotel, so I decided to go to a hospital to have it examined. I also realized that I hadn't called my wife to let her know that I was all right. When I dialed my home number, the line was busy.

What I didn't realize was that many of my friends and relatives were calling to see if I had been shot. The first news reports earlier in the day had identified Tim McCarthy, who had been injured, only as "Agent McCarthy." This led to a great deal of confusion, since there were three Secret Service agents in Washington at the time named McCarthy, two of them named Dennis. When I finally got through to H.M., she already knew that I was okay because she had called the office and had seen me on the tapes of the shooting being broadcast over and over by the television networks. She had been out shopping when she heard the news. By the time she got home, the phone had begun to ring constantly.

I told H.M. that I had hurt my neck and would be going to Fairfax Hospital, not far from where we lived, to get it checked. First, however, I had to go to the FBI Washington field office to make a formal statement about the shooting. We agreed that I would call her when I was finished there, and she would meet me at the hospital.

I rode to the FBI field office at Buzzard Point in Washington in the motorcade that took Hinckley there from police headquarters. He was three cars ahead of the one I was in.

As we drove through the Washington twilight, I thought about all the times I had ridden along those same streets protecting presidents, vice-presidents, kings and prime ministers. Now, ironically, here I was helping to escort a man who had just shot the President and three other people.

My statement to the FBI was concise. It described what had happened from the moment I left the ballroom after Reagan's speech until I dived on Hinckley outside the Hilton. After signing it, I called the Secret Service's Washington field office and requested an officer to drive me to the hospital and another to go to the hotel and pick up the Secret Service car I had left there. My neck was so stiff by this time I could hardly turn my head, and I didn't want to try to drive the twelve or thirteen miles to Fairfax Hospital.

H.M. had all the paperwork taken care of when I arrived. I spent the next two hours having X rays taken of my neck and back. Luckily, they showed there was nothing seriously wrong. The doctor told me the stiffness was a result of a strain and would cure itself in a few days. He said, "Go home, have a couple of stiff drinks, and make love to your beautiful wife."

We got home at 10:30, more than fourteen hours after I had left to go to work. It had been a very long day and probably the most eventful one of my life. But it wasn't over yet. I had a personal crisis to face. One of the messages on my answering machine was from an attorney in Annapolis, Maryland, whom I suspected my wife had been seeing. When I heard the message asking H.M. if I was the agent who had been shot at the Hilton, I almost exploded. I threatened to call him right back and confront him, but she talked me out of it. I was still very much in love with H.M. and didn't want to believe that she was being unfaithful to me. I was trying hard to overcome our marital problems, but she didn't seem willing to change the way she was living. I slept very little that night, thinking about the message on my answering machine and what it might mean. I knew I had to find out.

The next morning, I went to work as usual. When I got to the office, Robert Powis, the special agent in charge of the Washington field office, called me in to find out if I was all right or if I needed to take some time off. Since all the other agents in the office had gone on twelve-hour shifts to handle the details of the investigation, I didn't feel right about asking for what I considered a special favor. While part of me was screaming that I needed some time off, I kept telling myself, *If everyone else can take it, so can you.*

For the first few days after the shooting, I blamed myself for not having done enough or reacted fast enough. I was trying to keep up with everyone else, but I was having a great deal of difficulty concentrating on my work. I began to think that I might have acted like a coward outside the Hilton. Then I started watching the televison tapes of the shooting. From one angle I saw my hands blocking one of the cameras as the third shot hit Tim McCarthy. From another I could see myself diving through the air and landing on Hinckley. It was then that I realized I had started my dive as the second shot was being fired and that, until then, my view of the gun had been blocked by the cameras.

So I couldn't have reacted any faster. I had done what I had always hoped I would do in such a situation.

After everyone in the office had reviewed the tapes over and over, my fellow agents began congratulating me for what I had done. I was embarrassed by all of the attention, but I also was proud of the way I had reacted and appreciated the things my co-workers were saying. I felt proudest when another agent came to me and said, "Denny, you have had your moment of truth."

All Secret Service agents wait their entire careers for that moment, but only a few ever face it. Most retire never knowing for sure if they would match up to what is expected of them, although I believe most would.

The morning after the shooting, I tried to call the Annapolis attorney who had called my house the night before. He wasn't in his office that day, so I left my name with his secretary and asked that he call me the next day at my office. When he returned my call, I was so angry I began to tremble. When I told him who I was and asked why he had called my house on Monday, he very calmly told me that he had never met H.M., but was making the call for his roommate, a pilot for the same airline that H.M. worked for.

When I hung up, I knew my marriage was finished. On Thursday, H.M. left on a three-day working trip. She would be flying back and forth across the country, leaving me at home alone with my thoughts and fears. Friday morning, on the way to work in heavy rush-hour traffic, I found myself totally depressed. I should have turned around and gone back home, but I didn't. When I drove into the garage at the Washington field office, I sat there in my car for a few minutes and pulled myself together, or so I thought. However, as soon as I went upstairs Don Huycke, the agent who shared the office with me, saw that I seemed to be sitting there in a daze. Another agent came into the office, and when he noticed my condition, he went to get Powis. Then a supervisor came in and said we would have to work twelve-hour shifts Saturday and Sunday and on into the following week without any days off, and I exploded.

"No," I said, "no, I can't do it. I need some time off. My world is falling apart, and I can't take it. I won't do it. In fact, I'm going home right now."

I stood up, closed my briefcase, and walked out of the room. As I half walked, half ran down the hall, Powis came around the corner looking for me. He asked me what was wrong. I started to tell him the same thing I had said in the office, and found I couldn't control my voice. Embarrassed, I turned and walked out of the building, got into my car and drove home. I didn't know what I was going to do. I thought I was heading for a nervous breakdown.

When I got home, the phone was ringing. It was Powis, checking to see if I was all right. He told me that Ike Hendershot and Karen McLaughlin would be at my house shortly. They were two agent friends who knew about my problems at home. They arrived a few minutes later and stayed with me most of the day. Another friend called my minister, Tom McCusker, and told him what had happened. The minister also came to my house and stayed for a while.

It was the roughest day of my life.

Late that afternoon, Ike had to leave since he would be working a midnight shift and had to get some sleep. Karen lived just down the street from me and, after Ike left, she suggested that we go to her house and have some lunch. After eating, we talked for a while and drank a couple of beers. I went back home feeling a little better. I will never be able to repay Ike, Karen, and many other Secret Service friends for the care and concern they showed me during this period.

It was three weeks until I went back to work. I didn't know if I would be charged with sick leave or annual leave, and I really didn't care. I just knew I had to have some time away from the Secret Service. As it turned out, the service granted me administrative leave, so the time off didn't count against my personal leave.

When H.M. returned, she told me she had decided to take a vacation by herself. A few weeks before the shooting, she had arranged to go on a barefoot sailing cruise with a bunch of pilots and other flight attendants, and had planned to tell me shortly before they left. She claimed there was no romantic involvement in the trip, though she would be sailing the Caribbean in a small boat. The marriage counselor couldn't believe she would plan such a provocative trip while we were trying to rebuild our marriage, but H.M. could see nothing wrong with the trip. I told her I was going away too, with or without her. She decided not to go on her trip, and arranged instead for us to go on a windjammer cruise together. I enjoyed the sailing, but H.M. got sick one day during rough weather and later associated the whole trip with that day. When we returned home, we both knew that the end of our marriage was at hand, but we were having trouble making a final decision.

H.M. suggested that we separate for the summer, continue to see the marriage counselor, and have lunch once a week. Then, she said, we could sit down together in the fall and see if we had made any progress.

I refused. My two sons from my first marriage would be visiting me most of the summer, so I would have little time to date anyone, and I knew most women wouldn't be willing to go out with me anyway unless I was legally separated. So I demanded a legal separation. I told H.M. we could still have a talk in the fall, but I wanted to be free for the summer. If we decided in the fall that it wasn't going to work out, we could count the separation toward the year waiting period required by Virginia law before a divorce can be granted.

The legal separation began on June 9, 1981. Two days later I left Washington to visit Susanne and Gene Blankenship, long-time friends who lived in Fort Lauderdale, Florida. I got five sorely needed days of rest, but as soon as I returned, I was right back in the middle of the Hinckley case.

In mid-June, I began meeting with four psychiatrists who had been hired by the government to evaluate Hinckley's mental condition at the time of the shooting. During our first meeting at FBI headquarters, they spent two hours grilling me. I was the only person who had been with Hinckley constantly during the first hours after the shooting. The doctors wanted to know if he had been nervous, if he had been sweating or trembling, or if he had shown any signs of disorientation or confusion. I went through the whole story with them, giving them every detail I could recall.

The psychiatrists could tell from my account that I didn't believe Hinckley was mentally ill. They were gathering information to rebut an insanity plea that everyone expected Hinckley's lawyers to enter for him. A team of psychiatrists hired by Hinckley's family was working to establish that he'd been insane at the time of the shooting, but they never interviewed me, knowing I was a prosecution witness. The government psychiatrists told me they felt that I would make an excellent witness against a plea of insanity.

A few days later, I met with the assistant United States attorney who was in charge of the prosecution's case. I went through the whole story again with him, and he told me I would probably be called as a prosecution witness when the trial started.

I testified at a preliminary hearing, but when the trial finally began after several delays, I was called to the witness stand to testify only about Hinckley's arrest. After the assistant U.S. attorney led me through the step-by-step arrest procedures we had followed, the defense attorney asked only one question: Had Hinckley offered any resistance?

"None whatsoever," I answered.

When the psychiatric portion of the trial began, I was not called back. I believe this was a mistake on the prosecution's part. My testimony might have helped since I think the jury might have sympathized with a layman's assessment of Hinckley's mental state. There is no way to know if I am right or wrong, but obviously the government didn't have as strong a case as the Justice Department thought, because Hinckley was found not guilty by reason of insanity.

Early in the summer after the shooting, I was transferred from the Washington field office, where I had been assigned for four years, to the Secret Service's Liaison Division, and assigned to work at the State Department. I had applied for the liaison office opening along with eighty-five other agents. I guess my behavior during the assassination attempt helped me to get the job, but however I got it, I was happy about the change. It meant that only rarely would I have to work the streets again.

During the three and a half years that I spent at the State Department, I sometimes got the feeling that I was little more than the highest-paid messenger in the U.S. government. Part of the job involved getting the necessary visas for Secret Service personnel who were going overseas with the President or Vice-President or to advance a White House trip. I would arrive at an embassy with a handful of passports to be stamped and stand in line with young kids working for Washington law firms or corporate offices who were there for the same reason. The only difference between us was that most of them came on bicycles, while I drove a government Buick and was being paid several times more than any of them.

Much of the Liaison Division's job involves public relations work with other government agencies and with the general public. It is an important job, because many people have their only personal contact with the Secret Service through the liaison office, and as a result form their impression of all agents. Besides, being there kept me off the campaign trail during the 1984 primaries and general election.

As a young agent twenty years earlier, I had been eager to get into the thick of every campaign, to be on the road with the presidential candidates. Now I was eligible to retire just two months after the 1984 presidential election. There were a lot of young agents in the service itching to be assigned to protect one of the candidates.

I was happy to let them have the job.

CHAPTER 6

Life in the Secret Service

I was born in Baltimore, but grew up in Falls Church, Virginia, one of Washington's older suburbs. After serving three years as an enlisted man in the Army, I returned home and attended Lynchburg College, also in Virginia, where I met and married my first wife, Shelby. I graduated in 1962, at the age of twenty-seven, with a degree in business administration and economics. I began working for the Treasury Department's Bureau of Accounts in Washington, supervising a bunch of little old ladies who were counting the months until they could retire. The job was one of the most boring experiences of my life, but I had been married only three years, had little savings, and felt obligated to keep it until I could find something I liked better. In the summer of 1963, I decided to apply to the Central Intelligence Agency, figuring it had to be more exciting than the Bureau of Accounts, when fate intervened in the form of the Treasury Department team in an interdepartmental tennis league. The Secret Service is part of Treasury, and my doubles partner in the league that summer was an agent. When I told him of my plans to apply to the CIA, he suggested that I try to get into the Secret Service instead.

After more than a year of examinations, interviews, and a complete investigation of my background, I was hired in Washington, but required to move to Omaha at my own expense to start to work. My first day on the job was November 22, 1964—exactly one year to the day after President Kennedy had been killed in Dallas.

The Secret Service of today is quite different from the original organization. The service was established in 1865 as a small Treasury Department police force to combat counterfeiting, which had become a major national problem during the Civil War. Secretary of the Treasury Hugh McCulloch first proposed forming an anticounterfeiting force during a meeting with President Abraham Lincoln on April 14, 1865. Lincoln authorized McCulloch to set up the unit.

Ironically, the discussion was one of the last official conversations Lincoln had. That night, he was shot by John Wilkes Booth while attending a play at Ford's Theatre in Washington.

Three months later, on July 5, 1865, the Secret Service Division of the Treasury Department went to work. It consisted of a chief with a squad of ten men, but their duties didn't include protecting the President, even though Lincoln had been killed because the city policeman assigned to guard him wasn't at his post when Booth pulled the trigger. The assassinations of President James A. Garfield in 1881 and President William McKinley in 1901 also failed to result in the establishment of a federal protective force for chief executives of the country. Finally, in 1906, Congress passed a bill authorizing the Secret Service to guard the President.

It was also in 1906 that a President traveled outside of the

United States for the first time in history. President Theodore Roosevelt, the first Chief Executive to have formal Secret Service protection, made a trip to Panama, accompanied by the two agents of the newly formed White House detail. By 1918, when President Woodrow Wilson left for the Paris Peace Conference following World War I, he had a detail of ten agents. The number of agents assigned to the White House had increased to thirty-seven by the time the United States entered World War II.

In 1922, at President Warren G. Harding's request, Congress authorized the Secret Service to establish a uniformed White House police force called the Executive Protective Service. This force, now called the Uniformed Division of the Secret Service, today guards the White House and adjoining executive office buildings, along with the Vice-President's house and all of the foreign embassies and diplomatic missions in Washington.

In a very real sense, however, the birth of the modern service can be traced to about 2 P.M. Washington time on Sunday, December 7, 1941, when Secret Service Chief Frank J. Wilson got a call at his Washington home from Mike Reilly, the assistant supervising agent of the White House detail.

"Chief," Reilly said, "the Japs have bombarded Pearl Harbor."

Prior to that day, which President Franklin D. Roosevelt would designate "a date which will live in infamy," security around the White House had been fairly lax by today's standards. Visitors came and went pretty much at will. Taxicabs drove right up to the front door. Even the flag on the roof told the world whether the President was at home or not. It flew only when Roosevelt was in the White House and wasn't raised when he was traveling or staying at his private homes in New York or Georgia.

Chief Wilson, the equivalent of today's Secret Service director, had for over a year been planning the security measures that would be necessary if the United States entered the war that had been raging in Europe since the fall of 1939. Within hours after the attack on Pearl Harbor, he began putting his plans into effect.

As Chief Wilson describes in his book, *Special Agent*, written with Beth Day, "My greatest fear was that a Nazi undercover agent or saboteur might be willing to sacrifice his own life if he could assassinate our President. I immediately decided to intensify to a high degree the protection extended to him."

While General George C. Marshall, Secretary of State Cordell Hull, Secretary of the Navy Frank Knox, and other top government officials converged on the White House for urgent meetings with Roosevelt, Chief Wilson started putting his security plans in force.

He immediately canceled all leaves and days off for Secret Service agents, putting the entire force on twelve-hour shifts and doubling the number of agents at the White House. Agents quickly confiscated the press credentials of all Japanese, German, and Italian journalists in the country. It also fell to the Secret Service, as the Treasury Department law-enforcement unit, to freeze the assets and confiscate the records of all German, Japanese, and Italian firms with offices in the United States.

Wilson's most immediate concern, however, was Roosevelt's personal safety.

By the evening of December 7, a company of previously selected Regular Army troops from Fort Meyer, Virgina, across the Potomac River from Washington, was patrolling the White House fence. Immediately inside the fence was the White House police force as a second line of defense, and inside the building, nearest the President, were Wilson's special agents. It would have taken a tremendous amount of firepower to get through this triple layer of defense, but Chief Wilson was more concerned about less conventional ways of getting to Roosevelt.

The biggest concern was the possibility of an air attack. Because of the Pearl Harbor raid and the German blitz against London, air raids seemed to be on everyone's mind. By the Monday following the Japanese attack on the U.S. fleet in Hawaii, Wilson had Army anti-aircraft batteries set up on the roof of the Treasury building next door to the White House and a District of Columbia Fire Department engine company stationed between the two buildings. In retrospect, neither Germany nor Japan had any means of launching such an attack on Washington, but then, until the day before, no one had thought Japan could attack Hawaii, let alone sink several battleships in the process.

The weeks following Pearl Harbor probably were the busiest time in the history of the Secret Service. As Chief Wilson recounts in his book, "From the time of our entry into the war and for a period of four months thereafter not one Secret Service agent was able to take a single day off. Without exception, all of us worked Saturdays, Sundays and holidays until I felt that the situation was under good control."

Many of the practices and procedures established during those hectic days by Wilson and his men, all long since retired, are still being followed by the Secret Service in the 1980s.

Wilson arranged for the use of a secluded railroad siding track if it became necessary to move President Roosevelt from Washington secretly and promptly. A train was the most effective means of getting the President away from Washington in the 1940s. Today, with Soviet nuclear missiles a half hour's flight time from the White House, an Air Force Boeing 747 loaded with enough communications equipment to command and control the vast American nuclear arsenal remains near the end of the runway at Andrews Air Force Base with a flight crew on duty and ready to take off at a moment's notice. Should a president ever have to use this "doomsday plane," it will be up to the Secret Service shift on duty at the White House when the warning comes to get him there in time.

Prior to the Japanese attack on Pearl Harbor, the President didn't have an armored car. FBI Director J. Edgar Hoover had one and offered it to Roosevelt when the war began, but Chief Wilson made other arrangements. When the Treasury Depart-

ment nabbed Chicago gangster Al Capone on an income-tax eva-
sion charge in 1932, his heavily armored touring car had been
seized. It had been in storage for nearly a decade in a government
garage. A few days after Pearl Harbor, Chief Wilson, who had
been one of the federal agents primarily responsible for convict-
ing Capone, ordered the gangster's car brought to the White
House for Roosevelt's use until a new armor-plated car could be
built for him. Wilson also ordered an armored railroad car for
Roosevelt from the Pullman company, specifying three-inch-
thick bulletproof glass windows.

All White House Secret Service agents, policemen, and members of Roosevelt's staff were issued gas masks, and a mask was
attached to the President's wheelchair so it would always be
within his reach.

A survey by Army engineers requested by the Secret Service revealed that the closest and best place to establish an air raid shel-
ter for the President, his family, and top advisers was in Vault 1
beneath the Treasury building. To make room for the President,
$700 million in silver dollars, $1.8 billion in gold certificates, and
$7 million worth of opium and other drugs that had been stock-
piled for wartime use were moved to another vault. On Monday
December 8, the day after the Pearl Harbor raid, the Secret Service stocked the vault with twenty-four cases of bottled water,
two hundred pounds of food, and twelve beds, as well as first-aid
kits, a portable toilet, tables, chairs, and dishes. A second vault
was soon turned into an operations center and equipped with
telephones, desks, a surgical table, drugs, and other emergency
equipment.

Construction was begun on a 761-foot-long zigzag tunnel, 7
feet wide and 7 feet high, connecting the White House and the
basement of the Treasury building, although there was never a
need to use the tunnel to protect President Roosevelt from an air
raid.

Chief Wilson's wartime protective measures also resulted in

several other changes around the White House that endure. A much heavier and higher iron fence, the one through which hundreds of tourists still photograph the building daily, was installed around the grounds. The two streets adjoining the White House grounds, East and West Executive Avenue, were closed to traffic, reopened later, and closed again after Mr. Reagan was shot.

A few days after Pearl Harbor the Secret Service suddenly found itself with yet another responsibility that continues today. As Chief Wilson recounted in his memoirs, he was talking with Roosevelt one day in mid-December when the President matter-of-factly told him, "The Prime Minister—Churchill—is coming over for a series of conferences. There'll be plenty of work for your outfit, Frank."

While Secret Service agents had guarded a few well-known visiting foreign dignitaries prior to that time, Roosevelt's casual remark thrust the agency into an entirely new role. As President Roosevelt predicted, it has been "plenty of work," but forty-five years and thousands of visitors later, no foreign official being guarded by the Secret Service has ever been harmed while on American soil.

At 5 P.M. on Christmas Eve of 1941, Franklin D. Roosevelt and Winston Churchill spoke to some twenty-eight thousand people gathered on the South Lawn of the White House. Their somber messages were broadcast to the world by radio.

Although few people in the crowd knew it at the time or would have recognized its significance, that Christmas message was a landmark in the field of security. For the first time ever, the leaders of the two principal democracies in the world were addressing their constituents from behind an armored podium.

In addition to protecting Roosevelt, the Secret Service had its other primary mission to consider when the war began—protecting United States currency. Several million dollars in U.S. currency was in Honolulu banks when Japanese bombs began falling on Pearl Harbor. As soon as the extent of the military disaster there was known, it became evident that there was little to stop Japan from invading and capturing the Hawaiian Islands. To ensure that the Japanese didn't get their hands on the money, the Treasury Department ordered the Secret Service to destroy it.

Chief Wilson sent Agent Art Grube to Hawaii with orders to get the money out of the banks and burn it. Borrowing mail sacks from the Post Office Department, Grube gathered the bills from the banks and with a military police escort took it to the Oahu Crematory, where seven large lots of cash were reduced to ashes.

On Christmas Eve, as if he and his agents didn't already have enough to do with Churchill in town and twenty-eight thousand people about to be let onto the White House grounds, Chief Wilson got a call from Archibald MacLeish, the librarian of Congress, asking about how best to safeguard the original Declaration of Independence and other priceless historical documents. Although the Secret Service had no legal responsibility for the documents, Wilson immediately recommended that they be taken to the government's gold depository at Fort Knox, Kentucky, and stored there. On Christmas Day, the chief assigned his executive aide, Harry E. Neal, to handle the transfer. In addition to the signed copy of the Declaration of Independence, the other documents to be moved included the original signed copy of the Constitution, the original Articles of Confederation, the original texts of Abraham Lincoln's Gettysburg Address and Second Inaugural Address, a parchment copy of the Magna Carta, and a three-volume original Gutenberg Bible.

Three Secret Service agents took the four cases containing the priceless documents from the Library of Congress to Union Station in an armored truck on December 26. The train trip to Kentucky was made in total secrecy overnight and the material was deposited in a vault at Fort Knox shortly after noon the next day. Chief Wilson had even thought to make arrangements with the Bureau of the Mint to have the time locks on the gold vaults set so they could be opened on Saturday when the documents arrived.

Wilson notes in *Special Agent*, "Only five people in Washington and two at the gold depository in Fort Knox were aware that these historic documents had been secretly transferred to what I considered the safest place in the United States."

Chief Wilson was without doubt the father of the modern Secret Service, and many of the precedents he set for the service in those fast-paced days of late 1941 and early 1942 remain the cornerstones of presidential protection in the 1980s. But the service has undergone many other changes since he retired as chief in 1946.

It wasn't until July 4, 1951—eighty-six years after the first Secret Service agents went to work—that the service was given the job of guarding the President permanently. Prior to that time, the duty had been reviewed annually by Congress as it considered the Treasury Department's budget for the year.

When President Harry S Truman signed the bill, he quipped, "Well, it's wonderful to know that the work of protecting me has at last become legal."

When I went to work for the Secret Service on November 22, 1964, it had just been subjected to one of the most intensive inquiries in history following the assassination of President John F. Kennedy, and was about to undergo major changes. I was one of the last two agents hired under the "old system," as it was prior to the Warren Commission's exhaustive study of the assassination. There were only 350 agents at that time, but Congress was about to increase the service's size greatly according to the commission's recommendations. In January of 1965, two months after I began, 50 new agents were hired, and by the end of that year nearly 200 additional men were on the job. The force has continued to grow over the past twenty years, reaching almost 2,000 agents today.

Despite the changes that were instituted, the service still clung to many of its traditions. When I arrived for my first assignment in Omaha, one of the first questions my supervisor asked was whether I owned a hat. When I said no, he told me to go buy one, because all Secret Service agents wore hats. I still don't know why, but I suspect it was because J. Edgar Hoover required all his FBI agents to wear hats. With all the new men coming in over the next few years, the tradition soon fell by the wayside, however, and I haven't seen an agent in a hat in years.

I reported to work in Omaha with no formal training at all. I would learn to be a Secret Service agent on the job, and I soon found out that in small field offices like Omaha's, life in the Secret Service bore little resemblance to the way "G-men" were portrayed in the movies.

But I was eager to learn and, like all young agents, I had dreams of uncovering a million-dollar counterfeiting ring. Years later, as a senior agent in the New Orleans field office, I did help break up such an operation, but my first "case" in Omaha was less than earthshaking. It might be called "The Great Coin-Counterfeiting Caper," or "Whatever Happened to Rookie Agent McCarthy's Bullets?"

A newspaper distributor for the *Omaha World Herald* had been harassing the agent in charge of the office, Dick Roth, for a month to do something about someone who was dropping slugs instead of dimes into one of his street-corner vending machines. Since he only sold about ten papers out of the rack each day, the slugs were robbing him of most of his profit from that corner. Because techically it was a counterfeiting operation, the local cops—not wanting to be bothered, I suspect—had sent the newspaper distributor to our office. Finally, Dick got tired of listening to the guy's complaints and ordered us to stake out the corner, find out who the culprit was, and arrest him. Unfortunately, it was late February and very cold.

Nevertheless, the next morning at 5 A.M., your intrepid federal agents were lurking in the dark streets of Omaha, watching a newspaper rack. We took all the dimes out, so we were sure it was empty. Then, each time someone bought a newspaper, we ran to the machine after the buyer left and opened it to see if there was a dime or a slug inside. After two or three mornings of this, we had spotted our man.

Now our problem was how to apprehend him. After he "bought" his paper each morning, he boarded a city bus. Since we couldn't stop him until after we had removed the evidence from the rack, we would have to follow the bus and arrest him when he got off. We also needed the bus driver as a witness.

We made arrangements with the driver for us to follow the bus the next morning. He would signal us when the lone passenger who had gotten on at our corner left the bus. Our plan was working brilliantly until our man got off at a stop on the other side of town. The driver gave us the signal, but instead of waiting at the corner, the bus began creeping slowly down the street. While my partner arrested our suspect, I went running down the snow-covered street to stop the bus and get the driver to confirm that the counterfeiter actually had boarded his bus on the corner where we had observed him "buying" a paper with a bogus coin.

What I didn't know was that the bullet pouch on my belt had somehow come open, and I was dribbling ammunition into the slush along the street as I chased the bus. A more experienced agent would simply have gone to a gun shop, which would have been easy to find in Omaha at that time, and bought himself some more bullets. But when we got back to the office, I dutifully told my supervisor that I had lost them.

He sent me back out to find them.

After an embarrassing hour or so of searching up and down the busy street at midmorning, with several people keeping a wary eye on me, I found all but one bullet before I gave up.

When we took the case to the local United States attorney, he almost threw us out of his office. He wasn't about to waste his time, he said, on a $2.60 counterfeit-coin case. At the insistence of the newspaper distributor, however, we took the case to the county district attorney, who did prosecute. The suspect, who was a punch press operator, was convicted, received a $100 fine and six-month suspended sentence, and lost his job.

There were only three agents assigned to the Omaha field office while I was there. The office was responsible for all of Nebraska and Iowa, an area of 140,000 square miles that includes scores of small towns and a large portion of a major Indian reservation. Due to the size of the territory we had to cover, I spent much of the time on the road, investigating counterfeiting cases, interviewing people for other field offices or Secret Service headquarters, and investigating stolen and forged government checks.

In the early summer of 1965, I had three cases that took me from the southeast corner of Iowa to the northwest corner of Nebraska, a distance of nearly fifteen hundred miles in a week. The last of the three cases took me to the Rosebud Indian Reservation, which dips into Nebraska from South Dakota, to find an Indian woman named Pearl Yellowhorse. She had reported that a sixty-dollar government check had been stolen from her. It was our job to investigate the report. The senior agents in the office warned me not to go on the reservation without an Indian policeman. I thought they were just playing another trick on the rookie, but I later found out that, for their own safety, white federal agents didn't go snooping around the reservation alone. Being young and eager at the time, however, I drove to the reservation post office, identified myself, and asked where Mrs. Yellowhorse lived.

The directions I got were something like, "Go five miles west, take a right, go five more miles, take a left at the fallen tree, cross a creek, go fifteen more miles . . ."

When I finally found the place, it turned out to be one of the most broken-down shacks that I have ever seen. There were about a dozen naked children and fifteen skinny dogs running around a front yard of dirt that was packed as hard as cement and without a single blade of grass. An Indian man came out of the house. I asked him if this was where Pearl Yellowhorse lived. He said yes, but didn't volunteer any further information. I asked if she was at home. He said, no, he hadn't seen her in six weeks. But when I asked if he knew where I could find her, he told me to go back to town, to a certain bar, and she would be sitting in the third booth on the left drinking a beer.

I didn't believe him, but having driven as far as I had, it was worth a try. When I walked into the bar, there were four Indians sitting in the booth the man had described. I asked if anyone knew Pearl Yellowhorse. One of them looked up from her beer and said yes, she was Pearl Yellowhorse. She had no idea, however, what had happened to her lost check, or if she did, she wouldn't tell me.

It was a long drive back to Omaha.

All of the field offices are larger now than they were in the early 1960s, but agents assigned to them still spend thousands of hours a year investigating hundreds of similar reports.

There was little regard for the personal lives of agents when I first joined the service, although the situation had improved by the time I retired since there was a larger selection of agents. I had been required to move to Omaha to start work, but six months later I had to return to Washington for six weeks to attend the Treasury Department's law-enforcement school. Shelby was pregnant with our first child at the time, but that made no difference to the Secret Service. Then, in August 1965, I was ordered back to Washington to join the Intelligence Division, which was being expanded as the result of a Warren Commission recommendation. Our first son was born on August 14, but I was given only a two-week extension of my reporting date in Washington. Shelby never forgave the Secret Service for making us move halfway across the country with a month-old baby. Nevertheless, after the nine months we spent in Omaha, I knew I had found a career in the service.

Despite the problems the move caused us, I was glad to get

Left to right: President Johnson, McCarthy, and Bess Abell, then social secretary to Mrs. Johnson, on the South Lawn of the White House (September 1968).

President and Mrs. Nixon in a Savannah, Georgia, motorcade.
McCarthy is at front left (October 1970).

Friendly crowd nearly overturns golf cart upon President Nixon's arrival at San Clemente. McCarthy, crouching, attempts to hold back crowd (October 1972).

President Ford and McCarthy, then a member of the Secret Service ski team, in Vail, Colorado (December 1976).

Left to right: McCarthy, Mike and Gayle Ford (the President's son and daughter-in-law), and a ski patrol member at Vail (December 1976).

The "body watch" at the rear entrance of the Washington Hilton Hotel minutes before the attempt to assassinate President Reagan. John Hinckley is third from the left (March 30, 1981).

President Reagan leaving the Hilton after his speech, seconds prior to the shooting. Hinckley is hidden behind a police officer (March 30, 1981).

Security forces moving in to seize Hinckley (March 30, 1981).

McCarthy and other security personnel surrounding the now docile
Hinckley (March 30, 1981).

President Reagan with, *left to right,* McCarthy, Jerry Parr, Ray Shaddick, and Timothy McCarthy in the Oval Office (July 1981).

President Reagan questions McCarthy on details of the shooting incident, in the Oval Office (July 1981).

back to Washington as one of about fifteen agents selected in the fall of 1965 to form the nucleus of the expanded Intelligence Division. Prior to that time, the division had been small and antiquated, comprising only five or six agents. Over the next few years, it would grow from this initial corps to a full-scale, computerized section of the service. I remained with the division full-time until February 1968, when I joined the White House detail.

Much of the Intelligence Division's work in those days dealt with potential danger to the President from protesters against the Vietnam War. I posed as a student on the campus of the University of California at Berkeley several times in order to gather information on the antiwar movement, much of which was centered there. This wasn't truly "undercover" work, in that I never registered for classes and didn't spend long periods of time on the campus. Mostly it consisted of wearing jeans and standing on the periphery of anitwar rallies just listening, trying to pick up bits and pieces of information that, over a period of time, would enable us to anticipate what was going to happen at demonstrations against the President.

I had no personal bias against any of the antiwar demonstrators. The great majority of them were average college students, some of whom were just out for kicks, but most of whom truly believed the war was wrong. I felt that the militant leadership of organizations such as the Student Nonviolent Coordinating Committee (SNCC), Students for a Democratic Society (SDS), and the Weathermen, who gave us the worst time, were truly dangerous, however.

The largest demonstration we ever dealt with involved thirteen thousand antiwar protesters outside a Democratic party fundraiser for President Johnson at the Century Plaza Hotel in Los Angeles. The demonstrators were led by nearly two thousand hard-core members of SNCC, SDS, and the Weathermen. Before it was over, two hundred people were injured, including about seventy-five demonstrators who were hurt seriously enough to be hospitalized.

Prior to the protest, the Los Angeles Police Department had an informant who was telling them everything that was going to happen. A secretary whose brother had been killed in Vietnam, she had successfully infiltrated one of the most active antiwar groups. She took detailed notes at strategy sessions leading up to the demonstration and passed them to the L.A. police. Based on her information, we were able to go into federal district court and obtain an injuction against the demonstration. We hit the leaders with cease-and-desist orders just as the demonstration began. While the court orders didn't stop them, it threw their plans into turmoil and, I feel, reduced the violence.

It was a constant battle of wits with the antiwar demonstrators. The Intelligence Division was always in the thick of the action, trying to outthink and outguess the protesters. The potential for mass violence was always just beneath the surface. We often had to move the President through hostile crowds and protect him without violating the constitutional rights of citizens who disagreed with his policies. This often involved such safety measures as using alternate motorcade routes, but mostly it came down to trying to find out what the protesters were going to do, and then sitting down and trying to figure out what we could do, legally, to counter their plans. Keeping our actions within the law was always the first consideration, and I don't know of a single time when the Secret Service crossed the legal line during those turbulent years.

But sometimes, no matter how much intelligence we had or how much advance planning had gone into an event, it wasn't enough to anticipate the unexpected—or to keep it from scaring the hell out of us when it happened.

First Lady Pat Nixon was a strong supporter of Washington's "Summer in the Parks" program—a joint effort of the city and the National Park Service geared toward keeping inner-city kids off the street and out of trouble. One hot summer night, she decided to go from the White House to the Washington Monument grounds, where an estimated fifty thousand people were gathered for a free Stevie Wonder concert. She had no sooner arrived on stage, smiling and waving to the huge crowd, when the audience, made up mostly of black kids, began chanting, "Kill Mrs. Nixon! Kill Mrs. Nixon! Kill Mrs. Nixon!"

The First Lady just stood there, stunned, but District of Columbia Mayor Walter Washington, who was on the stage also, turned and asked us to get her out of there as quickly as we could. The stage was surrounded by Washington and park policemen, but there was only a small security detail with Mrs. Nixon, and it took us a few minutes to get the cars up to the stage to get her back to the White House.

Of the hundreds of news photos I have appeared in over the years while guarding various dignitaries, one of the few I saved is from that night. It shows me standing directly behind Mrs. Nixon with my hands on two chairs that were behind her. I was ready to throw the chairs out of the way and jerk her off the back of the stage if necessary.

It was the best thing I could think of at the time.

We got Mrs. Nixon safely away from the monument grounds that night, but the worst situation with demonstrators I ever encountered came during President Johnson's 1967 trip around the world. I was the intelligence advance agent in Australia, arriving almost three weeks ahead of Johnson. We knew that large anti-war demonstrations were going to occur when the President arrived in Sydney. The police were very good and pinpointed everyplace where there would be trouble when Johnson arrived. Still, the protesters threw paint on Johnson's car and on several of the agents around it. Some of the demonstrators tried to lie down in the street in front of the motorcade. They had to be carried out of the way by agents and Australian security men.

The local authorities in Sydney had reserved the front row of a section of the parade route for children and handicapped people so they could see Johnson. As the motorcade approached, some of the demonstrators in the rear of the crowd began pushing forward to try to get into the street and stop Johnson's car. The Sydney cops went after them on horseback, catching the kids and people in wheelchairs in the middle. Several American and Australian security people, including myself, saw what was happening and waded into the crowd to try to keep the kids and old people from being crushed. None of them was hurt seriously, but it was very close to being a disaster. It was the only time I ever wanted to jump in and beat the hell out of some of the demonstrators.

As usual, the danger—this time to innocent bystanders, instead of the President—arose, reached a frantic peak, and died in less than a minute.

The intensity of such trips puts a severe strain on the personal lives of Secret Service agents. Advancing an overseas presidential or vice-presidential trip often keeps them away from home for four to six weeks at a time. During this period they are under constant pressure to make all the necessary security arrangements, often without the cooperation of the host country's authorities.

The Secret Service hires well-educated men and women from stable backgrounds with no criminal records, trains them to react instantly to almost any situation, and then assigns them to jobs that take them away from normal lifestyles much of the time. This puts great pressure on the average family. In most cases, the spouses of agents frequently find themselves playing the roles of both husband and wife at home. Many aren't capable of coping with the strains brought on by their spouse's job, and so the trouble begins.

I was thirty years old when I was hired by the Secret Service and well on my way to becoming the average family man with a wife and a mortgage. When President Johnson left Brisbane to go on to Asia and the other members of the advance party returned to the United States, I had to go back to Sydney to interview an American prisoner who had been jailed there for threatening Johnson's life.

While I was waiting for the flight from Brisbane to Sydney, a young woman sat down beside me in the airport. I was extremely tired and the last thing on my mind was meeting anyone. As it turned out, however, we spent most of the next four days together. She later moved to the United States and I saw her during the frequent trips President Nixon made to California. She knew I was married, and once or twice brought up the possibility of my getting a divorce.

I suppose I was trying to have it both ways, but I had two young sons, and I wasn't ready to give up my family. We slowly drifted apart, and she eventually married a man in California, where she still lives—happily, I hope. Looking back on it now, though, I can see that this was the beginning of the end of my marriage to Shelby.

I don't know what it is about foreign trips that makes some Secret Service agents go a little crazy. Neither do I know anything about the national statistics on American men fooling around when they are away from their wives. But for agents, especially on foreign trips, the opportunities are abundant and the temptations great.

The agents are thousands of miles from home, almost always staying in the best hotels, dealing with some of the top officials of the host countries who frequently live life in the fast lane themselves. If we decided to have a short, intense affair, we somehow felt shielded from being discovered. It was as if, for that short period, we weren't married or were living on another planet. It was something to ease the pressure and the stress, we rationalized. As I look back on it, that wasn't a valid excuse, but I still believe something is needed to relieve the stress and strain of such trips. I don't know what the answer is or why many agents seem to be able to resist the sexual temptations while others aren't.

Having once gone astray with the affair that began in Australia,

I found it easier and easier to get involved with women as I traveled around the world.

However much extramarital activity there is on the part of some of the Secret Service agents, the job is a lot more work than fun. Members of the White House detail, who guard the President, and other details assigned to protect senior government officials or presidential candidates work in eight-hour shifts, seven days a week, every day of the year. The partying that sometimes goes on while traveling does so only when agents are off duty.

It doesn't matter if the President is staying in a hotel suite, at a friend's home, or at his own—agents are on duty around him at all times. And they are deadly serious about their work. Even at the White House on Christmas morning when the President and his family are opening their presents to each other, there is a Secret Service detail on duty just outside the family's private rooms. Maybe that is the kind of thing that makes some agents go a little overboard when they are off duty hundreds or thousands of miles away from home.

Still, the glamorous resorts of the world don't seem so glamorous when you are standing in a deserted hotel corridor at four o'clock in the morning or having a verbal battle with the man you are supposed to be protecting, as I once did with Henry Kissinger on the beach at Acapulco.

After Kissinger left office as Secretary of State in January 1977, President Carter assigned a Secret Service detail to him for six months, primarily because he had been so deeply involved in the politics of the Middle East. The huge demonstrations the service had been contending with in the late 1960s and early 1970s were rare by then, but international terrorism was becoming a factor in all security planning.

I was assistant agent in charge of the special detail, and I liked Kissinger. He is the most intelligent man I have ever met, and it was a real challenge to match wits with him, although I usually lost. He could, however, be a real pain when it came to security matters. He challenged us from the start to see how much he could get away with.

Carter had requisitioned all of the smaller armored cars in the Secret Service motor pool for use by the White House, because he didn't want to use the huge black limousines that Presidents before and since have always used. Carter's preference for the smaller cars left us no choice but to assign one of the black monsters to Kissinger.

The first morning we arrived at his house to pick him up, Kissinger took one look at the car and stopped short.

"I am not going to ride in that thing," he said.

I politely told him he had no choice.

He became furious and threatened to walk, take a cab, anything rather than be driven around Washington in something that faintly resembled a tank. I can't say I blamed him, but I stood my ground. "We're here to protect you," I told Kissinger, "and this is the only vehicle available for us to do our job." He finally relented and got in, but ordered us to park half a block from his house every morning when we came to take him to his office in downtown Washington.

Kissinger also made a game of trying to get the agents on the detail to carry his briefcase. As Secretary of State, he had had plenty of aides to take care of such trivial matters, and he didn't want to be bothered with them now even though he was no longer in office. He would get out of the car and leave the briefcase on the backseat, or walk away from a meeting without it. But it was our job to protect him, not act as his personal servants, so every time this happened I would say, "Excuse me, Dr. Kissinger, but you forgot your briefcase."

We would then stand there until he went back to get it.

This battle of wills was more of a game than a real problem, but on a trip to Acapulco, I was forced to stand my ground on a much more serious issue. Kissinger and his wife, Nancy, were staying at a luxurious private house on the beach. Mrs. Kissinger suggested that they go swimming, but there had been recent reports of sharks in the water and signs were posted warning swimmers to stay out of the bay.

Kissinger asked me if I would put agents in the water with him and his wife if they went swimming. I figured it wasn't part of the Secret Service's duty to become shark bait for a former secretary of state, so I told him, "Dr. Kissinger, if you're concerned about sharks, my suggestion is that you don't swim in the bay."

I didn't forbid him to do what he wanted, but I wouldn't commit my men to go into the water with him. We dueled over the issue for several minutes until I finally told him, "If the sharks come on this beach, my agents will fight them, but they aren't trained to fight sharks in the water."

He finally dropped the issue, but my stay in Acapulco was anything but a vacation.

Kissinger soon forgot about such run-ins, however, and I think we emerged from our six months together with a lot of respect for each other.

More than a year after his detail was discontinued, I was advancing a reception that Vice-President Walter Mondale was attending for the Prime Minister of Japan at the Japanese Embassy in Washington. There were about a hundred guests, and as I waited with the top Japanese security people at the embassy entrance for the Vice-President and the Prime Minister to arrive, Kissinger came in. When he saw me, he stopped and asked, "Mr. McCarthy, what are you doing here?" I told him I was in charge of the security advance. With a grave look on his face, Kissinger turned to the Japanese security people, shook his head, and said, "Your Prime Minister is in serious trouble."

After taking three or four steps toward the door, he turned back with a big grin on his face and told the startled Japanese, "I was only kidding. Mr. McCarthy is a very good man."

That kind of moment rarely occurs with the powerful people protected by the Secret Service, however. Most of the time, agents must create their own diversions from the pressures and the boredom of the job.

One instance of occupational levity was created several years ago by Jim Kalafatis, an agent in the New York field office who invented a fictitious "Agent Capezzi." The New York office is the largest in the service, requiring several hundred agents to deal with the United Nations, the foreign heads of state who visit the city regularly, and the counterfeiting aspects of organized crime. No one could possibly keep track of all of the agents there, so for months Kalafatis and other pranksters drove the supervisors crazy with Agent Capezzi. He got calls on the radio, filled out daily reports on cases he was investigating, applied for promotion—everything that could be done through the Secret Service's vast paperwork system. But no one ever saw him. Every time he was supposed to be at a meeting, someone would report that he was out on a case and couldn't make it back to the office.

Of course, the supervisors eventually figured out what was going on, but years later Capezzi's name still shows up on occasion in the service's internal newsletter. No one has written an obituary for him yet.

When President Nixon used to go to his friend Robert Abplanalp's private island off the Florida coast frequently, a favorite trick of the White House detail was to warn new agents of Abplanalp's good-natured, friendly, somewhat overweight Bahamian cook. The cook, the new man would be told, was always trying to talk agents into going to bed with her. He would be warned to be especially careful when on duty at the post in back of the house, adjacent to her kitchen, as she had been known to come out and try to coax agents into the basement with her when no one was around. It had been tried in the past, the new man was advised, so he should be forewarned.

The shift leader would purposely assign the new man to the back post after one of us had asked the cook to show the agent coming on duty where the emergency telephone was located in the basement. Would she please take him down and show him personally, the agent would ask. The cook was eager to cooperate with us, so we would position ourselves at good vantage points and wait for the action to begin.

Several times the cook practically dragged struggling agents into the basement in her effort to be helpful as they resisted mightily, determined not to be caught away from their post and in the basement with the "oversexed" cook.

Agents also sometimes unexpectedly stumble onto the practical jokes of the people they are protecting. Bebe Rebozo's house was within the Secret Service security perimeter around Nixon's house at Key Biscayne. One evening, Abplanalp was planning to spend the night with Nixon, but had been visiting Rebozo at his house. I was in charge of the shift that night and was in the command post when an alarm went off, indicating that someone was opening a door in one of the houses. I called the agent on duty outside and asked him who else was outside in the compound. He couldn't tell who it was in the dark but advised me on the radio that someone had come out of Rebozo's house and gone to the Nixon house.

Since I would need to know who it was for my log, I decided I had better go investigate. I walked to Nixon's house and went into the living room. I heard nothing so I walked through the house to a back bedroom where I could see a light. As I approached the bedroom, I saw Abplanalp standing at the foot of the bed staring at something. I glanced down and saw what appeared to be a woman's feet sticking out from under the covers.

I didn't know how anyone could have gotten into the compound without passing a security checkpoint, but I thought I had interrupted Abplanalp with a lady friend.

"Oops," I said, "excuse me, Mr. Abplanalp," and turned to leave.

"Wait a minute," he said. "Don't leave. I want you to be my witness."

He knew what I had seen and had guessed my thoughts. He grabbed my arm and led me back to the bedroom, where he pulled the covers back to reveal a mannequin in the bed. He had no idea how it had gotten there, but the next morning Manolo Sanchez, Nixon's valet, confessed to having played the joke.

There are pranksters on every Secret Service detail. One of them on the Nixon detail was Agent Pat McFarland, known as Farkie. We were aboard a military helicopter en route from Homestead Air Force Base near Miami to Key Biscayne once when Manolo was along with Nixon's big Irish setter, Timaho, on a leash. The dog was lying between Manolo's legs. As soon as we were in the air, Manolo settled back and dozed off for the short flight. The seats on the chopper were long benches down each side, and I was sitting directly across from Farkie and Manolo. I could tell something was about to happen when I saw a sparkle in Farkie's eyes.

He looked at Manolo, then at the dog, and began to smile. Without warning, Farkie began snarling very loudly, like a dog about to attack, and reached over and grabbed Manolo in the crotch. I never saw anyone wake up as fast an Manolo did. He was sure the big red dog had him by the balls, and the look on his face was one of pure terror. About two dozen people aboard the helicopter practically fell into the aisle laughing.

On another occasion, I was standing post on the bay side of the Nixon house at Key Biscayne. It was a beautiful day but boring as usual with no one else around. A few hundred feet away, I could see Chuck Rochner at his post. As usual, Chuck was dapper in white pants, a red shirt, and a blue blazer.

Since there was nothing else going on, Chuck seemed to be the perfect target for a little fun. He was casually strutting around his post when I called him on the radio. In a very serious voice, inflecting it with all the "security" tone I could, I told him I thought I had just seen someone moving around in the vicinity of his post.

He immediately began looking frantically around his area but naturally couldn't see anyone.

I began moving him from one location to another, suggesting that he look behind this tree or that bush. I was really enjoying myself as he kept coming back on the radio asking for more directions.

Finally, I started giving him a description of the mysterious "intruder."

"I think he has on white pants. . . . It looks likes he's wearing a red shirt . . . and a blue blazer . . ."

With that, Chuck shouted over the radio, "That's me, you stupid son of a bitch!"

He would have killed me if he could have left his post.

CHAPTER 7

Living with Lyndon (and Jerry and Jimmy and Others)

In addition to the public and their superiors, Secret Service agents must also deal with the personalities of the men they protect.

Lyndon Johnson holds the record for being the most difficult President to deal with on a personal basis. Before he was elected Vice-President in 1960, Johnson, as majority leader of the Senate, had been the dominant man in Congress. He'd been treated like a king on Capitol Hill. When he became President in 1963 after President Kennedy was killed, Johnson expected the same kind of treatment in the White House. Richard Nixon has often been accused of creating the "imperial presidency," but to those of us who saw both men from inside the White House, the title suited Johnson much better.

With his Texas-size ego, Johnson treated the Secret Service like hired hands on his ranch. Johnson never called an agent by name, and he didn't know the names of any except the three or four most senior members of the detail. His usual practice when he wanted something was to yell, "Secret Service," followed by some demand.

Occasionally, though, we were presented with an opportunity to get even.

Johnson had a dog named Yukie, who slept with him. One miserable, rainy night at his ranch near Johnson City, Texas, Johnson put the dog out in the middle of the night, screaming to the agent on duty outside, "Secret Service! Throw Yukie back in when he's finished."

As usual, there was no "please" or "thank you."

Yukie was a small, unfriendly mutt, and that night he got very muddy before he was "finished." Seeing this, the agent at the post just outside Johnson's bedroom was delighted to follow the President's orders, exactly. He quietly opened the door to LBJ's bedroom and threw the soaking-wet dog back inside. The next morning, the President awoke to find the silk sheets on his bed quite a mess. Afterward, we were told not only to put the dog back inside after he had been out, but to clean him up first.

I believe that because of Johnson's he-man image of himself, he resented having agents around him all of the time. He didn't like the idea of needing "protection" from anyone. Since it was Kennedy's assassination that had raised him to the presidency, Johnson was surely aware of the necessity for protection, but it must have grated on his ego.

After leaving office in 1969, Johnson demanded that his agents keep a "respectful distance." Even though he was no longer President, a detail continued to protect him until his death, just as former Presidents Nixon, Ford, and Carter will be protected by the Secret Service for the rest of their lives. Johnson's detail was more than happy to abide by his request, except they called it giving him "screaming distance."

Johnson liked to drive his own car, but couldn't do so except on the roads around his ranch while he was President. One morning not long after he left office and moved back to Johnson City, he decided to drive to his office in Austin, about sixty miles away. The agents on duty were maintaining the required "respectful" distance in a follow-up car when suddenly LBJ's car pulled to the side of the highway. As the detail watched through binoculars, still respecting the former President's privacy, they radioed back to the command post at the ranch the following description of his actions:

"The President has stopped his car beside the highway. . . . The President is getting out of the car. . . . The President is walking around the car. . . . The President is examining a tire. . . . The tire is flat. . . . The President just kicked the tire. . . . The tire refused to inflate. . . ."

After a "respectful" amount of time had passed, the detail drove up to help change the tire.

Before Johnson left office, however, there was no such thing as giving him "screaming distance." An incumbent president is never more than a few feet away from at least one Secret Service agent. This constant proximity can get on the nerves of both the Chief Executive and the agents who have to live with him. In the summer of 1968, after Johnson had announced that he wouldn't run for reelection and Senator Robert Kennedy had been killed while campaigning in Los Angeles, Secret Service headquarters took half of the White House detail and assigned these agents to other candidates of both parties who were running in the primaries. A group of relatively young and inexperienced agents from Secret Service field offices around the country were brought to the White House on temporary assignment to fill out the presidential detail. Most of these new men had never been around Johnson before.

One of the new members of the detail was posted one day, soon after arriving in Washington, at an elevator in the White House when Johnson came down from the family quarters on the second floor to go to his office in the West Wing.

Having been pumped full of "You're just a heartbeat away from the President," the new man was very anxious to do his job right and stay close to Johnson. As they walked toward the Oval Office, the agent was so close to Johnson that he was almost step-ping on the President's heels. After taking a few steps this way, LBJ turned around abruptly, almost causing his bodyguard to knock him down, and asked gruffly, "Who are you with?"

"The Secret Service, sir," the agent answered.

"I know that, goddamn it," Johnson said, "but who are you with [meaning which office or division]?"

Confused by this sudden turn of events, the agent blurted out, "I'm with you, sir."

With that, Johnson turned and started walking again, mum-bling to himself, "Goddamn, he's with me. Goddamn, I'm with him."

Every time they passed a White House police officer, Johnson would jerk his thumb over his shoulder toward the agent and say, "He's with me. I'm with him. Jesus Christ! Goddamn! He's with me! I'm with him!"

The White House cops got a good laugh out of the President's putting down the new guy in town, but the incident was typical of the way Johnson treated the men who were there to protect his life.

There were times when we had no choice but to resort to downright deceit to protect him.

When he was at his ranch, Johnson liked to pilot a speedboat that was kept by the Coast Guard at a nearby lake for his use. The Secret Service had three Donzi speedboats there for our use when the President was out on the lake. Two of our boats were fast enough to keep up with Johnson's boat, and the third, a red one, could run circles around anything else on the lake. All the kids around the lake knew how fast it was, and Johnson suspected it, so he was always challenging us to race him. For security reasons that should have been obvious even to Johnson, we had to have the fastest boat. But we were afraid that if we ever beat him in a race, Johnson would take our red boat for his own use. So we always let him win.

One day Henry Ford II was visiting the ranch, and Johnson decided to take him for a boat ride on the lake. We had the red boat tied up at the dock with the motor running and the hatch open to keep the engine cool, when Johnson and Ford walked out to the presidential boat. As they passed, the automobile company executive glanced down at the engine in our boat, nearly stopped walking, and said, "My God!"

We quickly signaled for him to keep quiet about the engine. Ford understood our "high sign" immediately, but not before LBJ became suspicious again and challenged us to another race.

Since discretion is the better part of valor in such situations, we maintained our perfect record by losing again, making the President very happy and keeping our boat at the same time.

Not all presidents are as difficult to deal with as Johnson was, but Jimmy Carter was never very popular with the service either. He never yelled and screamed at agents the way Johnson did. He just never said anything to them. It was as if they weren't even there most of the time.

I wasn't on the White House detail during the Carter administration, but a fellow agent related a story to me that shows the difference in personalities between Carter and his successor, Ronald Reagan. This agent was on the White House detail when Carter left office and Reagan moved to Washington. Shortly after the inauguration, he was on duty at the White House and escorting Reagan from the family quarters to the Oval Office.

Reagan began talking, and the agent immediately looked around to see whom he was talking to. There was no one else there.

"All of a sudden," he told me later, "I realized he was talking to me."

Carter rarely engaged in small talk with anyone, let alone Secret Service agents. It turned out that the coolness between Carter and the men on his detail was one of those Catch-22 situations, however. Carter thought the agents didn't like him, and the members of the detail thought the President didn't like them.

When he came into office, Carter continued Gerald Ford's efforts to sweep away the image of the imperial presidency that had developed during the Nixon administration, more through Nixon's staff than his individual style. Ford had begun the process on his first day in office by telling the country, "I'm a Ford, not a Lincoln."

Ford, a former Michigan congressman who owed his political success to a highly personal style, was very popular with the White House detail. He was friendly and easy to get along with, and agents who were close to him say he was exactly what he appeared to be—a nice guy trying his best to do one of the most difficult jobs in the world, which in his case hadn't even been sought. The agents on the detail at that time were more than happy to do whatever they could to make things easier for him.

While Carter also tried to erase the impression of a presidency far removed from the people, he did so in a different way—by remaining aloof from the Washington crowd. He tried to set the tone for his administration during his inaugural parade, when he walked down Pennsylvania Avenue from the Capitol to the White House instead of riding in a limousine. He discouraged his supporters from playing "Hail to the Chief," the traditional presidential song, when he spoke to large gatherings and wouldn't allow military bands to play it at official functions. And, as already mentioned, he told the Secret Service to get rid of the huge, black limousines at the White House and provide him with smaller cars.

Soon after he took office, Carter also complained to the Secret Service about the use of police sirens in motorcades around Washington. Word of this soon reached the Metropolitan Police Department and Park Police, both of which provide motorcycle escorts for presidential motorcades. A few days later, Carter gave a speech at the Washington Hilton Hotel. Afterward, the motorcade returned to the White House through a tunnel that runs under Dupont Circle on Connecticut Avenue. As Carter's car entered the tunnel, every motorcycle officer in the motorcade turned on his siren, creating an ear-splitting noise. As far as I know, Carter never said anything about the incident, but when the motorcade reached the White House, all the motorcycle officers had smiles on their faces.

It now appears, however, that President Carter and the Secret Service misjudged each other from the beginning. Members of the detail assigned to Carter at his home in tiny Plains, Georgia, since he left office consider it among the best jobs in the Secret Service. Carter is cordial, takes their advice on security matters, and lets them hunt and fish on his farm when they are off duty. On the other hand, few agents in the service are anxious to get assigned to Ford, not because they dislike him but because he attends many social functions and travels a great deal of the time, both of which can create a lot of work and many difficulties for the relatively few agents assigned to a former president.

The details assigned to other government officials are also small, so agents get to know the person they are protecting very well —sometimes well enough to make a joke at his or her expense.

When Kissinger was named director of the National Security Council in the Nixon administration, a small detail of three or four agents was assigned to him during working hours, which for Kissinger often meant twelve or fourteen hours a day. Despite the long hours, though, the agents assigned to Kissinger liked him and were generally on friendly terms with him. One day as the NSC chief was being driven to an appointment in Washington, the car got stuck in a traffic jam. With nothing to do as the car crept along, Kissinger struck up a conversation about security. The talk got around to terrorism, then just becoming a major concern of U.S. security officials. Kissinger asked the head of the detail what he would do if they were attacked by a band of terrorists.

Although the discussion revolved around a serious matter, the agent decided to test Kissinger's sense of humor.

"Well, Dr. Kissinger," the detail leader said in a serious tone, "you know that I carry a gun that has six bullets. I would probably get five of the terrorists, but my orders are not to let you be taken alive."

Kissinger looked at him in stunned silence for a few seconds and then said, "You're kidding, of course."

The agent assured Kissinger with a grin that he was joking and went on to explain what he would actually do if they were attacked.

Kissinger would have had no reason to know it at the time, but for about six months during his tenure as Secretary of State, his name, or at least one of his nicknames, was on the minds of many agents who had nothing to do with protecting him.

Preventing forgery of government checks and bonds is one of the Secret Service's major law-enforcement functions. A man cashed six thousand dollars' worth of forged U.S. savings bonds in Cincinnati, and a month later several more bonds from the same batch were cashed in Miami. Bank tellers in both cities described the man as resembling the Secretary of State, and photographs taken by a security camera at the Miami bank showed that their descriptions were accurate. Agents working on the case soon dubbed the suspect Dr. K. It took six months, but they finally caught the man in Boston after he cashed more than one hundred thousand dollars' worth of stolen bonds. Dr. K was convicted and received a ten-year sentence. Had he known about it, I'm sure the real Dr. K wouldn't have objected to the agents' borrowing his nickname.

While agents spend countless hours with famous people like Kissinger, they are expected to remain individually anonymous. The service wants the security details around such people to be highly visible for obvious reasons, one of which is to deter potential attackers. If there are a lot of guys with guns protecting a government official, it is less likely that someone will try to harm him or her. Individual agents, on the other hand, are supposed to maintain a low profile. Sometimes, however, no matter how hard they try they find their way into the limelight.

After former First Lady Jacqueline Kennedy married Greek shipping tycoon Aristotle Onassis, her Secret Service protection ended, but a detail continued to guard the Kennedy children. Following her marriage, the tabloid newspapers in the United States and Europe went crazy with stories about Mrs. Onassis. One of them reported that she had a "secret lover" and all the others quickly tried to top the story. Before long, one of the papers published a photograph of Mrs. Onassis talking to a man on the Onassises' private island. The picture was accompanied by a story claiming that the man in the photo was her mystery lover. Several other pictures appeared showing her with the same man—whom the scandal sheets dubbed Mr. X—at different locations around the world. Nearly every week there would be some new "revelation" about the supposed secret lover.

Had the tabloids done even a minimal amount of research, they would have discovered that the man they were frantically trying to photograph with the former First Lady was Secret Service agent Jim Kalafatis, a member of the detail that guarded her children. Jim, who was later to gain a place in Secret Service lore for inventing the fictitious Agent Capezzi in New York, still has some of the pictures of himself as the mysterious Mr. X. Of course, if the papers ever identified him, it would have ruined their story, not to mention giving Jim the opportunity to sue their pants off.

While Kalafatis and a number of other agents are well known within the service for their practical jokes, none of them comes close to matching the reputation of the late Brooks Keller.

Simply stated, Brooks is a Secret Service legend.

He was wealthy enough not to need the job, or any job for that matter. Perhaps since every male member of his family for generations had died before reaching fifty years old, he just decided to pack all the life he could into the time he had. When he died, at forty-nine, friends from all over the world came to his funeral. For years, when an advance team went to some relatively out of the way place in Europe, Asia, or Africa, the first question they would be asked by local security officials was whether they had known Brooks. His wide circle of friends included not only police and government officials, but also artists, actors, writers, and assorted other characters.

The parties Brooks arranged on the press plane and at hotels during presidential trips during the Kennedy administration were so popular that one day President Kennedy asked him to report to Air Force One. When he got the message, Brooks thought he had done something wrong, but Kennedy said he just wanted to meet Brooks and find out how he could get invited to some of those "wild parties" he'd been hearing about.

All of this didn't sit well with the conservative Secret Service hierarchy, and Brooks was frequently in trouble with his superiors. One of his most famous escapades took place when he was already in trouble with the New York field office. Brooks was in Europe on business. His supervisors decided he had lingered too long and ordered him to take "the next available transportation" back to New York. He checked and found that all the flights that day were booked, so the "next available transportation" just happened to be the liner *Queen Elizabeth 2*. Naturally, Brooks booked passage but neglected to inform the New York field office of how he would be crossing the Atlantic. When he showed up after the leisurely five-day cruise, he was given a thirty-day suspension without pay.

Since, unlike most of us, he didn't really need his government check, Brooks went off and enjoyed his unexpected vacation. When the thirty days were over, he reported back to the office and asked if he could possibly get another thirty days tacked on to his suspension. He was ordered to get back to work immediately.

Brooks was known as the most transferred agent in the service. Every time he got into trouble with a supervisor, off he would go to another post.

One of his earlier escapades took place while he was assigned to the St. Louis field office. The agent in charge of the office wasn't very well liked by the men he supervised. He always wore a hat, a practice Brooks used to drive the man nearly crazy. Brooks went to a haberdashery and bought two hats identical to the one his boss wore, except that one of the hats was a size larger and the other a size smaller. Then he began switching them with the agent's own hat. If it rained, Brooks would sneak the too-small hat onto the rack. When the agent in charge came out of his office to go to lunch, his hat wouldn't fit. When he mentioned it, the agents in the office told him they had heard that the high humidity in St. Louis sometimes caused people's heads to expand slightly. Then there would be a cool day and Brooks would place the hat that was a size too large on the rack. The cold caused the head to shrink sometimes, the agents told their supervisor. This prank went on for months before Brooks either tired of the game or was transferred. The agent in charge of the office never did discover what was going on with his hat.

In 1976, I was a member of Treasury Secretary William Simon's detail when he went to Moscow for trade negotiations with the Kremlin. As we arrived at Andrews Air Force Base to leave Washington, I was astonished to see Brooks. He had finagled his way into a temporary assignment on the Simon detail be-

cause on the way back from Moscow, the Secretary was scheduled to stop in London. Brooks was getting married and his fiancée was going to meet him in London, where some friends were
planning an engagement party for them. Brooks could easily have
paid for his own ticket to England, but it was part of his game to
get the Secret Service to transport him to whatever part of the
world he wanted to be in at any given time.

Before leaving for Russia, we were informed that the Soviet
government would no longer permit us to shop in a particular
Moscow store that was reserved for senior Soviet military officers.
This store was popular with agents because many of our friends at
home wanted us to bring them the brass Red Army belt buckles
that could be purchased there. For years, these belt buckles with
red stars on them had been the most popular souvenirs of trips to
the Russian capital.

Brooks paid no more attention to the Soviet bureaucracy than
he did to what he considered ridiculous Secret Service regula-
tions. When we got ready to leave Moscow, Brooks showed up at
the plane with armloads of boxes. We asked him what he had and
he began pulling out Soviet field marshal's hats, admiral's hats,
belt buckles, and an assortment of other Russian military para-
phernalia. When we asked him where he had gotten it all, he
said, "At the military store in Moscow."

He had convinced a Soviet government interpreter to go with
him to the store, where Brooks had posed as a field marshal in the
Red Army. With the interpreter doing all the talking, Brooks simply acted like he knew what he was doing and pointed to the various items he wanted. That he could have been thrown out of the
country if he had been caught—and gotten the poor interpreter
sent off to Siberia—only added to the fun.

Brooks's name was liable to pop up anywhere. I had been in a
bar in Manhattan one night for only a few minutes when the
phone rang. The bartender answered and yelled, "Is Brooks
Keller here?"

I told him that Brooks wasn't there, but I was a friend and would take the call. There was a woman on the phone, but when I explained to her who I was, she hung up without giving me her name.

Brooks had so many connections and friends in New York City that he could arrange almost anything. The supervisors hated to ask him for favors because they didn't want to be indebted to him, but sometimes they had no choice. This once enabled him to pull off a stunt the likes of which most of us can only dream about.

When Kissinger was Secretary of State, Mrs. Kissinger decided she wanted to see a certain Broadway play. The show was sold out, but Kissinger demanded that the service get him tickets. The New York field office supervisors tried everything they could think of, but there were no tickets to be had. They explained this to the Secretary, but he still insisted on going to the play. Even with all its official clout, however, the office failed to obtain the tickets.

Finally, Brooks was asked to see if he could come up with some tickets for the Kissingers. He said he would see what he could do, and within a few hours returned with tickets for two of the best seats in the house.

Normally when someone under Secret Service protection attends a play, seats are bought for agents to sit behind, in front of, and to the sides of the official they are guarding. But since Brooks produced only two tickets, Kissinger's detail, along with some of the supervisors from the New York office, would have to stand in the back of the theater.

That evening, the Kissingers arrived and went to their choice seats. Then, just before the curtain went up, in walked Brooks with a cape over his shoulders and a beautiful woman on each arm.

While the whole audience watched, they strolled down the aisle and took the three seats directly in front of the Kissingers.

The supervisors standing in the back of the theater must have been steaming, but they couldn't say a word to Brooks.

Most federal officials don't live the life that Kissinger did while he was in office, and most Secret Service agents certainly don't live in the style of Brooks Keller. The problems encountered by the agents assigned to the Reverend Jesse Jackson's presidential campaign in 1984 were much more typical, although Jackson's campaign did create more problems than usual.

When Jackson announced his candidacy for the Democratic presidential nomination late in 1983, he asked for and was granted Secret Service protection immediately, although the other Democratic candidates weren't assigned agents until just before the first primary in New Hampshire, in February 1984. Anticipating possible complications, many of the agents assigned to the Jackson detail weren't looking forward to it, but at first the campaign staff was easy to work with and most of the agents liked the candidate once they got to know him.

Often it is the little things that presidents or candidates do that agents remember the best. Jackson impressed his detail on Christmas Day by calling all their families to apologize for making the agents miss Christmas at home.

Soon after the first of the year, however, things began to fall apart. Jackson's staff had no experience in running a national political campaign. They began making spur-of-the-moment changes in the events and even in the cities Jackson would visit the next day. No security detail can be effective under such circumstances, and a constant battle between agents and Jackson staff members developed.

A sign soon appeared in the campaign's Secret Service operations center. It read TO KNOW HOW A CIRCUS WORKS, YOU HAVE TO WORK FOR A CIRCUS.

One of the agents on the detail got into a fist fight with one of Jackson's campaign workers and was immediately removed from the detail. The other agents assigned to Jackson began discussing doing the same thing, since the guy who got into the fight was now back in a field office somewhere while they continued to put up with all of the daily hassles.

Then Jackson decided to make an overseas trip, and the security problems multiplied. It got to the point where the agents in the operations center put up two more signs, one designating a DOMESTIC DESK and the other a FOREIGN DESK.

I got involved in this aspect of the Jackson campaign since, as the Secret Service liaison officer with the State Department at that time, I was supposed to secure visas for the agents who would accompany the candidate on the trip. The countries on Jackson's itinerary changed daily, and sometimes hourly. I would be on my way to an embassy to get visas, only to receive a call saying that Jackson wasn't going to that nation anymore.

One of the countries finally decided on was Cuba. At first the official I dealt with at the Cuban Interest Section in Washington was very suspicious of my application for visas. I went out of my way to convince him that our only interest was in having agents with Jackson and that the Secret Service wasn't trying to pull any tricks to get agents into Cuba. After a couple of days, the official became very cordial and cooperative, and the agents who went on the trip said the Cuban security officials were very cooperative while they were there.

Though it had nothing to do with Jackson or anyone on his staff, one of the most bizarre events of the 1984 campaign took place on a Jackson trip. The candidate was on a regularly scheduled commercial flight accompanied by his Secret Service detail. As usual, one of the pilots turned on the plane's public address system to make the routine announcement about altitude, airspeed, estimated time of arrival, and so forth.

When he finished, however, he apparently forgot to turn off the PA system.

In a few seconds, everyone in the passenger cabin of the plane heard the same voice come over the loudspeaker again.

"Well," the pilot said, "now that that's over, all I need is a cup of coffee and a b— j—."

Clearly alarmed at the sexual reference, one of the female flight attendants ran up the aisle to tell the pilots that the PA system was on and that the passengers could hear their conversation.

As she passed the section where Jackson and his entourage were sitting, one of the agents leaned into the aisle and said, "Don't forget the coffee!"

CHAPTER 8

An Impossible Task

Sooner or later, every presidential administration has its run-ins with the Secret Service. The service's job is to see that the President is exposed to as little danger as possible, which involves keeping him away from hostile crowds and screening those who will be close to him. This is fundamentally at odds with the aims of the President and his political advisers, especially during election years. They want maximum exposure to the voters and as many opportunities to press the flesh as possible.

Unless the White House decides to run a "Rose Garden campaign," keeping the President at the executive mansion most of the time and relying primarily on television, reelection campaigns therefore make for a continual battle between the Secret Service and the President's political advisers. Of course, the White House staff, and ultimately the President himself, have the final say about where he will go and when. The Secret Service, or any other security force in a democracy, can only make recommendations, but when these recommendations have been ignored in the past, the results have sometimes been tragic.

Providing absolute protection for anyone is an impossible task. No one recognizes this better than security men and the people they guard. Not long before he was killed in Dallas, President Kennedy remarked to his staff that no amount of security could guarantee his safety.

"If someone is willing to trade his life for mine," Kennedy reportedly said, "there is nothing anyone can do about it."

Mahatma Gandhi made a similar remark to the New Delhi chief of police shortly before his own assassination in 1948. In that case, there was no breakdown in security, however, because there was no security. Although the New Delhi police had a substantial amount of intelligence on a plot to kill Gandhi and urged him to allow the posting of guards around him, the Indian leader absolutely refused.

In Kennedy's case, the decision to ride through the streets of Dallas completely exposed was a political one made by the President himself. The trip to Texas in November 1963 was the beginning of Kennedy's campaign for reelection a year later. It was already apparent that conservative Arizona Senator Barry Goldwater would be the Republican candidate in 1964, but there was a serious split in the Texas Democratic party. Vice-President Johnson had carried Texas for Kennedy in 1960, but three years later the administration was in serious political trouble there. Texas Democrats at the time of the Kennedy administration were divided between the liberals led by Senator Ralph Yarborough and the anti-Kennedy conservatives led by Governor John Connally (who later switched parties and served as Secretary of the Treasury in the Nixon administration). Both factions were suspicious of Johnson, and Kennedy hoped to unite them in a two-day swing through the state.

The first day of the trip, November 21, 1963, went well. Huge, friendly crowds greeted Kennedy and Johnson in San Antonio and Houston. Security was a greater concern in Dallas. The November 22 edition of the *Dallas Morning News* carried a full-page advertisement, bordered in black, denouncing Kennedy for being soft on communism. A few weeks earlier, United Nations Ambassador Adlai Stevenson had been jostled by a crowd of angry conservatives after a speech in Dallas, and during the 1960 campaign a group of angry women had spit on Johnson and his wife, Lady Bird, for running with Kennedy. Dallas was a hotbed of rabid conservatism and Kennedy wanted to show that he wasn't afraid to enter the lion's den.

When the motorcade left Love Field for downtown Dallas, Kennedy's staff ordered the Secret Service to take the protective "bubble top" off the Lincoln Continental limousine, and the President himself waved off the agents who customarily rode on the car's running boards. This forced all of the presidential security detail to hang on to the follow-up car, a 1955 Cadillac nicknamed the *Queen Mary* because it weighed ten thousand pounds.

Because Johnson was along, there were two separate Secret Service details in the motorcade. The Kennedy detail was headed by Roy Kellerman. Rufus Youngblood was in charge of security for Johnson. Rarely do the President and Vice-President travel together, but the political situation in Texas made this a special occasion. Kennedy and Johnson were flying on separate planes, but otherwise the schedule called for them to be together almost constantly. At each stop, Johnson flew in first on Air Force Two, a propeller-driven DC-6, so he could greet Kennedy when he flew in aboard Air Force One, a Boeing 707 bought in 1962 as the first presidential jet and still in service today as the backup plane for a newer, but almost identical, 707.

Dallas Police Chief Jesse Curry drove the lead car of the motorcade, and Dallas County Sheriff Bill Decker and Secret Service Agent Forrest Sorrels rode in the backseat. Next came the President's open limousine, driven by an agent, with Kellerman in the front seat. Behind the limousine was the *Queen Mary* packed full of agents. Another open convertible followed, carrying Johnson,

Yarborough, and their wives along with Agent Youngblood. The remaining vehicles, a mixture of cars and chartered city buses, were for White House staff members, Texas politicians, and the press.

It's impossible to say whether agents riding on the limousine would have blocked the shot that killed Kennedy. Lee Harvey Oswald had to be an expert marksman to hit a moving target at such a range, but agents riding on the sides of the car would certainly have made his shot much more difficult.

When the shots rang out, Agent Clint Hill jumped off the *Queen Mary* and raced to the limousine, clambering onto the rear bumper just before the car sped away toward Parkland Hospital. The most famous photograph from that tragic day is probably the one that depicts Hill climbing over the back of the car while Mrs. Kennedy appears to be trying to get out of the car. What the picture doesn't show is that Mrs. Kennedy was reaching for a piece of the back of her husband's skull that had been torn away by Oswald's shot. Hill was attempting to get her back onto the seat and get himself on top of the President. Although he couldn't have reacted any faster and was the only agent to reach the limousine from the follow-up car, Hill blamed himself for many years for not acting quickly enough.

As Hill leaped onto the bumper, Kellerman shouted into his radio, "Dagger, cover Volunteer!" Dagger was Youngblood's code name and Volunteer was Johnson's.

When the motorcade reached the hospital minutes later, Kennedy was taken to Trauma Room 1. Youngblood took the Johnsons to an isolated room in the hospital and ordered the Vice-President to stay there. A lot has been written about what the agents did in the aftermath of the shooting; some of it, especially by Kennedy staff people, has been critical. For instance, Kennedy family friend William Manchester implies in his book *The Death of a President* that ambitious agents were scrambling to change their allegiance from Kennedy to Johnson even before

Kennedy was pronounced dead by Dr. Kemp Clark, Parkland's senior neurosurgeon, half an hour after the shooting. Although I didn't join the Secret Service until a year after the Kennedy assassination, I know that nothing could be further from the truth. The agents in Dallas had no more allegiance to an individual than agents do today. It was a question not of allegiances but of sense: Kellerman ordered his deputy, Emory Roberts, to take most of the Kennedy detail and augment Youngblood's much smaller group guarding Johnson while Kellerman himself, Hill, and one or two other agents remained in the trauma room and with Mrs. Kennedy.

Although half an hour passed before Kennedy was officially pronounced dead, he was inside a secure hospital room with agents and Dallas police officers guarding the door. It had been obvious from the moment he was shot that he was critically injured, and Kellerman knew that if the shooting was part of a conspiracy, Johnson was the next likely target.

Youngblood was operating under the same assumption. He refused to let Johnson leave the holding room in the hospital even to walk down a hallway to speak with Mrs. Kennedy. For once, Johnson didn't argue, although he sent Mrs. Johnson to comfort Mrs. Kennedy.

The decisions made by Kellerman and Youngblood during those frantic minutes proved to be the correct ones. As Youngblood noted in his book, *Twenty Years in the Secret Service,* "John Kennedy was dead. He was beyond the protective efforts of the Secret Service."

Lyndon Johnson, however, was very much alive and Youngblood intended to make sure that he would stay that way. At the moment Kennedy died, the presidency automatically passed to Johnson and the responsibility for presidential security passed from Kellerman's detail to Youngblood's.

Thirty-three minutes after Dr. Clark officially pronounced Kennedy dead, Youngblood had Johnson aboard the presidential plane. Former Air Force One pilot Colonel Ralph Albertazzie and J. F. terHorst describe the scene in their book, *The Flying White House:* "At 1:33 Dallas time, Love Field beheld a strange spectacle. Two unmarked police cars, led by a motorcycle escort, swept onto the airport concrete and raced toward Air Force One. Youngblood, physically shielding Lyndon Johnson in the lead car, recalls one of the most welcome sights he had ever seen— 'the big, gleaming blue-and-white jet, with UNITED STATES OF AMERICA painted along the fuselage above the long row of windows and the number 26000 gracing the tail rudder.' "

Some of Kennedy's staff later criticized Johnson's use of Air Force One immediately after Kennedy's death. Perhaps one can understand their feelings, but from a security standpoint it would have been utterly ridiculous for the new President to have returned to Washington on older, propeller-driven Air Force Two while Air Force One, with its superior communications equipment, was used as a hearse for the dead President.

As Albertazzie and terHorst describe the scene, Air Force One was sweltering. Youngblood, feeling he had Johnson in the safest place he could get him for the moment, ordered shades drawn across all the windows, just in case there was another sniper lurking somewhere at the airport.

According to *The Flying White House,* Johnson strode past the Kennedy bedroom at the rear of the plane shortly after he boarded and gave a curt order to Youngblood: "I want this kept strictly for the use of Mrs. Kennedy, Rufus. See to that."

Youngblood posted agents at both of the aircraft's entrances to augment the Air Force guards already stationed there. He ordered that no one be admitted without his permission and that the airplane was not to move until Johnson indicated he was ready to leave.

Meanwhile, at Parkland Hospital, Dallas city officials wanted to take charge of Kennedy's body for an autopsy. Mrs. Kennedy and the dead President's top aides refused. As Albertazzie and terHorst describe it: "With Kennedy's angry aides and the Secret

Service clearing the way, the 900-pound casket finally was rammed past the protesting officials and into the mortician's white hearse. Mrs. Kennedy darted into a jump seat beside the casket. [Kennedy's military aide, Brigadier General Godfrey McHugh, and the President's doctor, Admiral George Burkley,] squeezed in behind agent Clint Hill. With agent Andy Berger at the wheel, the hearse whipped out of the hospital driveway. . . ."

The casket was placed in the rear compartment of Air Force One, the section Johnson had ordered reserved for Mrs. Kennedy. Though it wasn't legally necessary for him to be sworn in, Johnson kept Air Force One on the ground at Love Field until Judge Sarah Hughes arrived to administer the oath of office to him. To Youngblood's relief, the new President gave the order to take off as soon as Judge Hughes left the plane followed by Sidney Davis, then of Westinghouse Broadcasting, who informed the rest of the press that a new President had taken office. Mrs. Kennedy sent word forward that when Air Force One landed at Andrews Air Force Base, she wanted the men on her late husband's staff and the members of his Secret Service detail to carry the casket off the plane.

The Warren Commission's investigation of the Kennedy assassination and the recommendations that resulted from it greatly changed the Secret Service, as I have noted previously. There have been four attempts on the lives of men under Secret Service protection since, none of them successful: Alabama Governor George C. Wallace was shot and paralyzed from the waist down while campaigning for the presidency in Maryland, there were two attempts against President Ford, and President Reagan was shot.

In at least two of these cases, however, luck played as great a factor as any changes in security procedure. Both President Reagan and Governor Wallace survived because the bullets that hit them didn't kill them instantly, and their Secret Service details were able to get them to excellent medical facilities within minutes.

While both Reagan and Wallace became more cautious after being shot, they both campaigned for the presidency again, exposing themselves once more to the possibility that someone would step out of a crowd and start shooting. From a security standpoint, President Carter's decision to walk instead of ride down Pennsylvania Avenue from the Capitol to the White House after being sworn in was completely foolhardy, but it made political sense to Carter. The service went along with his decision, despite the danger it posed, because it had to.

There have been other times, however, when the Secret Service has been forced to do the job Congress chartered it to do against the wishes of the administration. I found myself in such a situation in the spring of 1983.

For several months before President Reagan sent U.S. Marines and Army Rangers to Grenada, his administration had been engaged in a running war of words with that tiny Caribbean island nation. Reagan had made an issue of an airstrip being built on the island by Cuban workers. During a nationally televised speech, he had shown satellite photographs of the construction and claimed that the airport could be used by Soviet MiG fighters. The following day, the socialist Prime Minister of Grenada, Maurice Bishop, made headlines in the United States by saying in a press conference that Reagan had no need to use an American satellite to get a picture of the construction work since there was a medical school at the end of the new runway attended by seven hundred students from the United States. He also claimed that the new runway was being built strictly to encourage tourism.

Like most Americans, I was hardly aware of Grenada or its Prime Minister so I paid little attention to the exchange between Reagan and Bishop over the runway. However, as Secret Service liaison officer to the State Department, I received a call a few days later from the Washington police inquiring about the protection the Secret Service would be providing for Bishop, what assistance we would need from the police, and what the Prime Minister's schedule would be.

My work at the State Department included helping set up Secret Service protection for visiting heads of state, but I had no knowledge of an impending visit by Bishop. After several phone calls to Secret Service headquarters, I learned that Bishop was indeed scheduled to make an "unofficial" visit to Washington and Detroit. Foreign leaders frequently make visits to the United States without having any formal meetings at the White House, or with the State Department or members of Congress. In such cases, however, if the visitor requests protection from the Secret Service, it's usually granted.

Bishop apparently thought he could get some political mileage out of announcing his desire to improve relations between Grenada and the United States by meeting with Reagan and Secretary of State George Shultz. But the administration flatly refused his overtures and word went out from the White House that Bishop was to be accorded no official recognition whatsoever.

This caused a problem for the service. If we provided a protective detail for the Grenadian leader, wouldn't it constitute "official" recognition of his visit? However, if we didn't guard him and some nut shot him the United States would have an international incident on its hands.

Once again we came up with a compromise. A detail would be assigned to guard the Prime Minister under the Secret Service's *congressional* mandate to protect all visiting heads of state while they are on United States territory. That way, the White House wouldn't be according him official recognition.

So the Prime Minister of a country not much larger than the District of Columbia, a man who had publicly called the President of the United States a liar, was escorted around two major U.S. cities for a week by a full-scale Secret Service protective detail while the administrative branch of the government ignored his presence in the country.

CHAPTER 9

Battling the
White House Staff

As a member of the White House detail during the Nixon administration, I saw firsthand the extent of the power wielded by the White House staff. H. R. Haldeman, Nixon's chief of staff, was generally despised by the agents stationed in the White House. For five years, before he was forced to resign because of Watergate, Haldeman controlled everything in the White House except the Secret Service, and he repeatedly tried to find ways to exert his authority over the presidential detail.

His design specifications for a new Air Force One aircraft in 1972 illustrate his self-important attitude and his control over the Nixon White House. Except for the identification number painted on its tail section, the exterior of the new Boeing 707 was almost identical to that of the old plane that had served as Air Force One for a decade. However, Haldeman enlarged the section reserved for the White House staff and placed his own seat, a large swivel chair, where he could see everyone who entered and left the President's private compartment. His deputies, Dwight Chapin and Larry Higby, were required to keep a log of all presidential visitors, noting when they entered Nixon's compartment, when they left, and, if possible, what they discussed.

Since the interior space was limited, something had to give to make room for Haldeman's larger staff section. That something was a good part of the compartment reserved for the agents traveling with the President. The seats in the Secret Service section of the new plane were so close together we could hardly move once we had squeezed into them. These cramped quarters made life miserable on long flights. It was bad enough on the frequent five-hour flights from Washington to Nixon's house in San Clemente, but it was terrible on overseas trips nine or ten hours long. Haldeman couldn't have cared less about the comfort of the agents traveling with the President.

As it turned out, however, the First Family was also unhappy with the interior design of the new plane. In the previous Air Force One, the First Family's lounge was adjacent to the President's compartment; in the new plane, Haldeman had inserted the staff section between them. Therefore, each time Mrs. Nixon or one of her daughters wanted to go from the President's section to the lounge, she had to walk through the staff compartment. Julie Nixon Eisenhower was as unhappy with the layout as her mother was, and when the members of the White House detail heard about it, they enlisted her help. One of the agents on Julie's detail asked her to come back to the Secret Service section during a flight to show her how cramped we all were. She did, and apparently reported our plight to the First Lady.

I doubt that Haldeman would ever have changed the arrangements if word of the Nixon family's dislike of the new plane hadn't been picked up by the press and stories hadn't begun to appear in the Washington papers. It didn't take much investiga-

tive reporting for journalists who covered the White House to figure out that Mrs. Nixon didn't like her husband's shiny new
plane, because her office was calling the Air Force each time the
family was scheduled to fly to California or Florida requesting
that the old Air Force One, now supposed to be the backup
plane, be used. A few weeks after the stories appeared in the
papers, the White House sent a memorandum to the Air Force
that stated the first time the new aircraft went out of service for
maintenance, the President wanted the interior changed to match
that of the older plane. In his memoirs, Air Force One pilot Albertazzie noted that changing Haldeman's design back to the
original configuration cost $750,000. It was this type of arrogance
that made us despise Haldeman.

He was unhappy with the Secret Service throughout the 1972
reelection campaign. Though all the polls showed Nixon way
ahead of South Dakota Senator George McGovern, the Democratic nominee, Haldeman wanted more "spontaneous" crowd
support to appear on television news programs. Before a rally at
the Providence airport, he ordered the White House staff advance men to drop the crowd control ropes so several thousand
people could surge onto the runway and surround Nixon. Bob
Taylor, chief of the White House Secret Service detail, heard of
the plan and called it off. Crowd control was a security matter,
Taylor told Haldeman, and if the ropes came down he, Taylor,
would personally arrest Haldeman.

That put an end to the plan for the time being, but the next
day, at the Greensboro, North Carolina, airport, White House
advance people let the crowd through the ropes just as the presidential limousine returned for Nixon to board Air Force One.
The Secret Service had no idea this was going to happen. Several
hundred frantic Nixon supporters poured onto the tarmac. Secret
Service agents literally had to fight their way through the crowd
to get Nixon aboard the plane. I'm sure the advance people who
let the supporters through were following Haldeman's orders.

Haldeman didn't forget Taylor's threat to arrest him. Although Taylor had worked for Nixon off and on since Nixon was Vice-President in the 1950s, Haldeman managed to make life so unpleasant for Taylor that he left the Secret Service to become chief of security for former New York Governor Nelson Rockefeller.

The agents' animosity toward Haldeman was so violent that they talked among themselves about "getting" Haldeman. More than once, I heard frustrated members of the White House detail say that if there was ever a gunfight around the President, Haldeman had better get his ass down in a hurry or he might catch a stray bullet from a Secret Service gun. Such talk was never serious; I'm confident that no one would actually have tried to harm him physically, but it did indicate how intensely Haldeman was disliked.

The Nixon White House staff tried in other ways to use the Secret Service to further its own political goals. I was directly involved in one such incident during the 1972 campaign.

I was the lead advance agent for a stop in Cleveland. Soon after I arrived there, a White House staff advance man came to me and told me that he wanted two security checkpoints established through which the public would have to pass to get in to see Nixon. He told me to set up one checkpoint at the edge of the airport and turn away any "hippie types" who tried to get in to the rally. The second checkpoint, where I normally would have put one, could be the real one for screening those who hadn't been refused entry already, the White House man suggested.

"This is a public rally," I told the White House advance man. "The Secret Service cannot be a part of saying who can come in and who cannot. We can eliminate weapons, but we will not eliminate beads or beards."

I refused to be a part of such a blatant violation of the public's constitutional rights during a presidential election campaign.

After considerable argument, during which I held my ground, the White House advance team built their own checkpoint. They fashioned two "chutes" through which the public had to pass to get to the rally. One chute, however, led not to the rally site, but to a parking lot. White House staff members manned this checkpoint and sent potential demonstrators into the parking lot and straight-looking Nixon supporters into the rally.

A few days later, several people who had been turned away from the rally filed suit in federal court against the Secret Service for violating their First Amendment rights. The service, however, was able to prove that no agent had participated in the phony White House "security" checkpoint. In any such event, the Secret Service issues lapel pins to everyone who plays any kind of official role. The pins are different shapes and colors to enable agents to identify who is supposed to be where. Agents themselves wear pins so they can identify each other. At a rally where large crowds are expected, agents from nearby field offices are called in to assist the White House detail with security. Since many of the agents involved may not know each other, this system is used to help everyone to tell who everyone else is.

In court, the demonstrators who had been turned away by the White House staff were asked to identify the kind of lapel pins worn by those who manned the checkpoint. They described the pins that members of the White House advance team had been wearing that day.

I believe that if Haldeman had ever gotten control of the Secret Service and appointed a political director, we would have been asked to do a lot of questionable things. I would have resigned if this had happened, and I know many other agents who would have also. To my knowledge, no other administration before or since has tried to control the Secret Service the way the Nixon White House did.

The airport rally at Cleveland was only the beginning of my troubles. It marked the start of the longest motorcade a president has ever undertaken. The route was ninety miles long and ended in Youngstown, Ohio. We passed through two dozen different police jurisdictions on the six-hour trip.

As the senior advance agent for the trip, it was my responsibility to coordinate all of the security arrangements. With the help of local police departments and Republican party organizations, I borrowed nearly seventeen miles of rope to use for crowd control. I ended up with everything from thin nylon cord to some heavy hemp ropes normally used to moor ships on the Great Lakes. This still wasn't as much as we needed, so I bought slightly over four more miles of rope. Since it was for a campaign trip, either the Republican party or the Nixon reelection committee ended up footing the bill.

When I finally got all the rope I needed, I had to find fifteen hundred 55-gallon drums to hold it up, transport them to various locations along the motorcade route, and then persuade the local fire departments to fill them with water so they would be heavy enough to support the ropes. Each barrel then had to be sealed so a bomb couldn't be hidden inside.

At times I felt as if I was the logistics officer for the Normandy invasion.

While all this was going on, I was fighting another running battle with the White House staff, which was single-mindedly planning to keep antiwar demonstrators out of the range of the television cameras filming Nixon's trip. Ohio has traditionally been a Democratic state with hundreds of thousands of blue-collar voters, and many of them lived on the route along which the presidential motorcade would pass. The White House staff wanted the television networks to show thousands of these workers lining the streets to cheer the President instead of "hippie" demonstrators protesting the war. It wasn't the Secret Service's place to help them stage-manage such a massive event.

A few days before the President was scheduled to arrive—while I was arguing with the White House advance team about what kind of security checkpoints we would have at the airport—a

White House Communications Agency advance man came to me and said he had orders to put a Secret Service radio in the senior White House staff car for the motorcade. In other words, Haldeman wanted a Secret Service radio in his car so he could monitor our frequency and tell what was going on along the motorcade route. We had never done that before and I refused to allow him to install the radio in Haldeman's car. Bob Taylor, chief of the White House detail, backed me up when I told him what I had done. But I had an idea I hadn't heard the end of it.

When the motorcade assembled at Hopkins Airport in Cleveland, I found out that the White House had assigned a junior staffer to ride in the lead Secret Service car. I knew immediately what the White House was up to. The staff man would be able to listen to the Secret Service frequency in the car and relay—by walkie-talkie to Haldeman—the reports of the agents posted along the route. Since there was no time to argue about whether or not the staff man should be allowed to ride in a Secret Service car, I instructed all the agents in the vehicle to wear their earphones instead of turning up the volume on the car's two-way radio. That way, only the agents in the car could hear the Secret Service channel. Haldeman didn't get a single report from the service about what was going on along the route. There wasn't a thing the White House staff could do. We had outmaneuvered them again.

The service not only has to fight the political advance teams during campaigns, but also finds itself taking the blame every time the candidate declines an invitation. Of course, agents understand the staffers' predicament: They're inundated with requests from local supporters of their candidate for things he can't possibly do.

"Why can't the President do this?" and "Why can't the candidate go there?" are questions asked constantly by local officials and politicans trying to get all the political mileage they can out of the highly publicized visit. For the harried political advance people, the easiest way out of some of these requests is to take the local politician aside and tell him, in a very confidential tone, "The President would love to come to your horseshoe-pitching contest, but security won't allow it." Then the mayor or the judge can go back to city hall or the courthouse and tell his cronies that the President really wanted to come to the event, but there were "some security problems" that he isn't at liberty to discuss.

In reality, where a president or presidential candidate goes rarely has a thing to do with security. The decisions are nearly always based on political rather than security considerations and are made by the White House or the candidate's staff, not by the Secret Service.

Advance agents are concerned with things like the safest motorcade routes, whether there have been any threats against the President made by someone living nearby, how many agents will be needed to cover the different locations he'll visit, and the quickest route to the nearest medical facilities. Gathering all this information, typing it up in reports, and getting it back to the agent in charge of the White House detail in the time allotted can make for some very long days. It's not unusual for an agent on an advance assignment to work several twelve- to sixteen-hour days in a row before the President arrives.

This had been the case with the Cleveland airport rally and ninety-mile motorcade. When Air Force One finally lifted off the runway in Youngstown late that afternoon, I had a splitting headache. I went straight to the hotel and collapsed into bed. The next stop was somebody else's problem, although the routine would start all over again the next day as the advance teams leapfrogged across the country, always one step ahead of Air Force One.

While it rarely makes any difference to agents on the White House detail that "security" is often used as an excuse for the President's not going somewhere, they do mind when a presidential aide tries to take some of the heat off himself by blaming the Secret Service for something it had nothing to do with. I once had a run-in with President Nixon's press secretary, Ron Ziegler, over such an incident. Nixon was visiting John Connally's ranch in Texas. Connally was Secretary of the Treasury at the time. The Secret Service received a request from him not to allow anyone to use the private back road to his house while the President was there. Since the road was Secretary Connally's private property, we complied with his wishes and closed it.

Members of the traveling White House press corps complained to Ziegler about not being able to use the road. I don't know why they thought they should be allowed to use it—unless perhaps they thought it was a public road—but instead of simply telling them that Connally wanted the road closed, Ziegler tried to take the pressure off the politicians by saying that the Secret Service was responsible for closing it.

I happened to be standing nearby when Ziegler made these comments during a news briefing at the ranch. His remarks irritated me a little, but I couldn't say anything at the time. As the reporters continued to gripe about the road, however, Ziegler turned to me and said in a very authoritative voice, "Joe, come over here, Joe."

He was looking straight at me and pointing his finger at me, but I just stared at him. After he called me "Joe" again, I looked at him and said, "Ron, my name is Denny."

"Oh," he said. Then, very loudly, he asked me, "What's this about the press not being able to use the back road?"

"Ron," I replied, equally loudly, "you know very well the request to close that road came from Secretary Connally."

Ziegler walked over to me and said in a low voice he was just trying to get the press off his back.

"Fine, Ron," I said in a voice loud enough for the reporters to hear, "get the press off your back if you want to, but don't use the Secret Service as a scapegoat in the process."

I turned and walked away, leaving Ziegler to deal with reporters now even angrier because they knew he had lied to them.

On another occasion, I was playing tennis in Key Biscayne with television network correspondents Robert Pierpoint, Tom Jarriel, and Herb Kaplow. On the adjoining court, Haldeman, Ziegler, John Ehrlichman, and another White House staff member were about to start a game. Ziegler arrived a little late and had to cross the court on which we had already started to play in order to get to his court.

Anyone who plays tennis knows the court courtesy involved in this situation. One waits for a point to be completed and crosses behind the players when there is no action going on. Ziegler, who wasn't known for his courtesy in any situation, crossed right behind Jerrald and Kaplow while we were in the middle of a point.

"Ron," I shouted, "court courtesy calls for an 'Excuse me' for your interruption."

To everyone's surprise, he did say, "Excuse me." But the TV correspondents with whom I was playing were a little astonished at my challenging a member of the palace guard in front of them. Later Pierpoint remarked that even the journalists who cover the White House every day sometimes forget that the Secret Service doesn't work for the White House staff.

Top-level presidential aides sometimes seem to lose touch with what is going on in the "real world" outside the White House gates. Perhaps this is somewhat understandable since they work incredibly long hours, nearly always six days and frequently seven days a week. Because of their positions, anyone who wants to see them must come to them. When they do have to go somewhere it is usually in a chauffeur-driven government car. They don't have to answer to Congress because of the doctrine of executive privilege, and most of their houses are equipped with direct telephone lines to the White House switchboard so the President can reach them at any time of the day or night. This can be pretty heady stuff, but it is still amazing just how far out of touch with reality some of the Nixon White House staff got.

Laguna Beach, California, was more or less headquarters for the White House staff and press corps during Nixon's frequent trips to his home in nearby San Clemente. During the summer months especially, the town usually appeared as if it was about to be overrun by hippies. There were many shops run by bearded young men and braless young women who sold a variety of mod clothes, beads, psychedelic cigarette wrapping paper, and other items used by those whom the White House staffers called hippie types.

The daily grind of duties usually slowed down somewhat when the President was in San Clemente and, in fact, sometimes nearly stopped altogether when Nixon went into seclusion for two or three days to prepare for a major speech or to get ready for an overseas trip. During one of these slow periods in the summer of 1971, Dwight Chapin, then presidential appointments secretary, and several other White House staffers went out on a shopping spree in Laguna Beach.

Chapin, who seemed to be a rather nice guy without much of a personality, always maintained that well-groomed, typical all-American Nixon-staff look, complete with American-flag lapel pin. Along with the group of shoppers from the White House staff, he wandered into one of the hippie shops. As they were looking at the mod clothes, Chapin picked up a "far-out" hat and tried it on.

A bearded and beaded employee walked over to him and, in the spirit of putting on the square I'm sure, said, "Heavy, man, heavy."

Chapin took off the hat, weighed it in his hands, and said with utter seriousness, "Yes, I think you're right—it is a bit heavy."

The hippie clerk just looked at him in disbelief and walked away.

There were many nice, dedicated, hardworking people on the

White House staff during the Nixon administration, just as there were in the Johnson White House and on the staffs of the other three presidents with whom I worked during the twenty years I was a Secret Service agent. Because of my assignments at the time, I had more direct contact with the Nixon staff than I had with the others. Many of the lower-level members of the Nixon staff—people like Diane Sawyer, then Ziegler's secretary and now a CBS news correspondent—were pleasant to deal with.

Despite the reputation the Nixon White House got during Watergate, not all of the people who worked there were humorless. One of those with a sense of the ridiculous was Steve Bull, one of Haldeman's deputies. Bull never seemed to take himself or his job as seriously as most of the other senior staff members did. He was also a great practical joker, as I learned one night while on duty at a formal dinner in the White House State Dining Room.

Agents assigned to such functions are required to wear the same dress as the guests so they will blend in with the crowd more readily. I don't remember whom this particular dinner was in honor of, but the dress was white tie. My post was in front of some sliding doors that form one of the entrances to the dining room, in full view of the President and most of his guests. Bull was also on duty that evening and was standing near me. I assume he was as bored as I was by watching a hundred or so people eat.

About halfway through the dinner, he slowly moved over to me and whispered, "Denny, I hate to tell you this, but your fly is wide open."

My face must have turned as white as my formal tie. I couldn't decide what to do since so many people could observe my every action. While I couldn't abandon my post and leave the President unprotected, the tailcoat left my fly totally exposed.

I finally decided to make a quick turn, face the door, pull up my zipper, and turn back to the guests, hoping all of them would be too busy eating to notice my movement. As I turned and felt for my fly, I discovered, of course, that it was already zipped. I had fallen completely for one of Bull's pranks.

By the time I turned back and glanced over toward him, Bull was having a difficult time keeping a straight face.

Later he told me he had decided I "just looked too damn dignified" standing there in my white tie and tails. I tried for years to get even with him for that one, but I never got the opportunity.

CHAPTER 10

Protecting the First Family

Secret Service agents assigned to the White House detail also protect members of the President's immediate family. Agents consider this good duty because there are fewer pressures, or at least not the same kinds of pressure involved in protecting the President when he travels.

When members of the First Family move around the country they don't usually generate as much advance publicity or public interest as the President does when he takes a trip. While protecting family members, the Secret Service is more concerned about the possibility of a kidnapping than an assassination. I don't mean to imply that some nut might not try to kill a First Lady or the son or daughter of the President—the Secret Service is there to prevent that too—but preventing a kidnapping is always uppermost in the minds of agents protecting family members. In recent years, understandably, this concern has increased greatly with the growth of international terrorism. If a terrorist organization was ever to kidnap a member of the President's family, he would be under almost unbearable pressure to accede to the group's political demands, although no President could consider taking such an action. The Secret Service has devised a number of means to minimize the possibility of such an occurrence, but they cannot be discussed here for obvious reasons.

In marked contrast to the presidential detail, the difficulties of this job are usually caused by those the service protects rather than by those from whom they are being protected. More often than not the family members would much prefer that the Secret Service leave them alone. While they understand the necessity of protection, they don't like it. Needless to say, differing intentions often create considerable friction.

For nearly two years of my five-year assignment to the White House, when traveling, I was in charge of Pat Nixon's detail. She is a gracious and polite lady and endured a lot of heartache during her husband's long political career. However, like nearly everyone else I know who lived in the pressure-cooker world of the White House, she sometimes felt the need to get away from it all, including the ubiquitous men with guns.

Once, while the Nixon family was on an extended trip to San Clemente, Mrs. Nixon called me to say that she was going to Los Angeles for a few days to visit a longtime friend. It didn't take long for me to discover I was going to have a problem.

Mrs. Nixon said that she was going to visit her friend alone, and that she didn't want any Secret Service agents with her. Instead of being driven in a government car with me riding shotgun in the front seat—our usual procedure—she said she was going to ride to Los Angeles with her friend alone. If I insisted, Mrs. Nixon conceded, I could follow in another car, but she wouldn't allow any agents around her friend's house during her stay.

The First Lady's requests contradicted all the most elementary security procedures, so I told her I lacked the authority to comply and would have to check with my supervisor. She told me not to check with anyone, and to be ready to leave that evening.

That "order" put me in a delicate position. If Mrs. Nixon got angry enough at me, she could easily arrange to have me transferred from the White House detail. If I did what she asked, on the other hand, I might be placing her life in danger—not to mention the risk of getting fired by the Secret Service. There was no doubt in my mind about what I should do. As soon as she hung up, I dialed Bill Duncan, the agent in charge of protecting the First Family, and recounted the conversation. He told me not to worry; he would go over and talk to Mrs. Nixon.

A half hour later the phone rang. It was Bill calling to say that he had had no more success than I with the First Lady, whose mind was set on going to Los Angeles alone. Our only solution was to let Mrs. Nixon think she was getting her way while we contrived to do our job.

It was agreed that I would follow Mrs. Nixon and her friend in a Secret Service car. I was to be the only agent she would ever see, but Bill assigned a carload of other agents to follow far enough behind me so that Mrs. Nixon wouldn't know they were there, and close enough to arrive in a hurry in case there was any trouble.

We made the trip to Los Angeles that evening without incident. When we arrived, I escorted Mrs. Nixon into her friend's house and gave her a radio on which she could contact me and also the telephone number of the nearby hotel where I would be staying. I asked her hostess to call me every day to let me know that everything was all right. Meanwhile, the other agents, who weren't supposed to be there, quietly spread out through the neighborhood to watch the house.

It wasn't an ideal arrangement, but we had one thing going for us: The press thought Mrs. Nixon was at San Clemente. As far as we knew, no one except the President and the First Lady's immediate staff knew where she was.

Only one mini-crisis arose.

Mrs. Nixon's friend called me about the third day of the visit to say that the First Lady wanted to go downtown to a beauty parlor.

"Fine," I said, "but you'll have to give me time to call the Los Angeles field office and get a dozen agents out to your house."

The startled hostess asked why on earth I would have to do a thing like that.

"Because," I told her, "if Mrs. Nixon goes out, everyone in town is going to know she's here and you're going to have reporters and television crews all over your front yard."

That quickly put an end to Mrs. Nixon's plans to go public with her "secret" visit to Los Angeles.

After five days, I went to pick Mrs. Nixon up. She came out of her friend's home looking rested and relaxed. As we walked to the car, she turned to me and asked, "Mr. McCarthy, did you have any agents up here during the past five days?"

I just smiled at her and said, "Now, Mrs. Nixon, would I do a thing like that?"

I drove her back to San Clemente, with the carful of backup agents still following at a discreet distance.

Mrs. Nixon always wanted as little security as possible around her and more than once complained to the President about the number of agents assigned to her. She was also genuinely concerned about not creating problems for other people when she traveled around Washington or any other city.

I had never bothered to tell her that when we went somewhere in Washington outside the White House, a second car with several agents always followed us. One day, while I was taking the First Lady to an appointment, the follow-up car got stuck in heavy downtown traffic. The agent driving turned to me and said, "We've lost the trail car," and slowed down to give the other driver a chance to catch up with us.

Immediately, Mrs. Nixon leaned up from the backseat and asked, "What trail car?"

I quickly explained to her that the second car was along just in case we had a mechanical problem, because we didn't want her to be stranded somewhere. It was true up to a point. She seemed to accept the explanation, and soon our backup unit was in place again and we continued on to the First Lady's appointment. From then on, however, we were careful to refrain from mentioning the second car in her presence for fear she would complain to the President again about having too much security.

One of my regular duties while assigned to Mrs. Nixon was to escort her to her weekly beauty-parlor appointment at Elizabeth Arden, a few blocks from the White House on Connecticut Avenue. I accompanied her there so often that the staff expected me, and when I arrived there would be a comfortable chair and a cup of coffee awaiting me. One day when I was off duty, another agent accompanied the First Lady to her appointment. Never having been there before, he stood around awkwardly until one of the employees noticed him. "Oh," she said, gesturing to my usual spot, "you can wait in Mr. McCarthy's chair."

I took a lot of kidding from other agents when the story spread around the White House about having my own personal chair at one of Washington's swankiest beauty parlors, but I still appreciated the courtesy of the Elizabeth Arden staff.

The presence of a Secret Service detail can be especially intrusive for teenage and young-adult sons and daughters of presidents. Four of the last five presidents have had children in that age range while they were in office. The ever-present security makes it very difficult for these young people to go on dates, to go to parties with their friends, to do any of the things that average young people enjoy.

Protecting the older children of a President can also be difficult for the agents involved. If, for example, the young person they're protecting goes to a party where marijuana is present, it can be an uncomfortable situation for the Secret Service detail. Whatever their own personal views about smoking pot, the agents are, after all, federal law-enforcement officers.

And then there are the times when the younger members of

the First Family rebel and decide they will take matters into their own hands.

Before they were married, Luci Johnson and Pat Nugent attended a party at a private home in Washington one evening. As usual, Luci's Secret Service detail went along, but the agent in charge had agreed that the couple could go into the party while the detail remained outside—not unusual when the gathering is small and the guests are friends. In such cases, the family member has a method by which he or she can instantly alert the detail should there be a problem.

Luci promised to notify her agents of any change in plans and went into the party. The detail settled back to watch the house. Once inside, however, Luci and Pat decided it would be fun to sneak out a back entrance and have an evening on the town without the Secret Service. Later in the evening, after most of the guests had left, the concerned agents decided to check inside to see what was keeping Pat and Luci. The hostess told them the couple had left earlier and the remaining guests claimed not to know where they had gone.

This was no laughing matter to the agents involved. Needless to say, the blame would have fallen on them if anything had happened to Luci. They were outraged by the supposedly mature couple's disregard for security, but could do nothing except return to the White House and wait for Pat and Luci to return.

Some time later, the wayward couple returned to the White House in a jovial mood. The agents met them with expressionless faces and watched silently as Pat escorted his fiancée upstairs to the family's private quarters on the second floor.

When Nugent came back downstairs, seemingly unaware of having endangered the President's daughter, he was met by the agent in charge of her detail, who decided it was time to teach Pat a lesson. It so happened that this particular agent was known for his boxing prowess, although he was smaller than Nugent. Before Pat knew what was happening, the agent grabbed him by the front of his coat, lifted him up against a wall and explained the facts of security life to him.

Pat and Luci never tried such a stunt again.

As far as I know, President Johnson never heard about the incident. If he had, I suspect that one of two things would have happened. Either he would have fired the agent in charge of Luci's detail, or he would have administered one of his Texas tongue-lashings to his daughter and future son-in-law. My guess is that it would have been the latter.

One might argue that a young couple in love and about to be married deserve a night out alone every once in a while without the Secret Service. Unfortunately, however, in today's world a round-the-clock security detail is one of the prices children of presidents must pay for living in the White House.

Luci Johnson had a streak of her father's Texan independence and was a rebel about security from the time the family moved into the White House. She would jump into her car and go roaring out of the White House gates, leaving her detail behind. After this had happened a couple of times, the head of her detail simply confiscated her car keys. After that, she didn't go anywhere without her agents.

As it often turns out, however, both she and Pat later became close friends with the men assigned to protect her. Before her marriage to Pat, a Roman Catholic, Luci decided to convert to Catholicism. She asked Bob Kollar, one of her agents to be a sponsor. Bob worried that assuming a role in the private life of someone he was protecting could be misinterpreted by the press, so he went to Rufus Youngblood, head of the White House detail, for advice. As Rufus relates in his memoirs, he told Bob, "It's a personal decision for you and I don't need to tell you that she's paid you one of the highest compliments she could. But for professional reasons, I think you should respectfully decline." Bob agreed and when he explained his reason for declining, Luci understood and agreed also.

When Luci and Pat were married in the summer of 1966, it fell to her Secret Service detail to get them away from the White House reception following the ceremony and to their honeymoon in the Bahamas without a horde of news people tagging along. Rarely do newlyweds have such expert assistance making their getaway.

The new Mr. and Mrs. Nugent were smuggled away from the reception through one of the underground tunnels that connect the White House and the Treasury building next door. Luci was provided a blond wig and carried luggage with the initials E.K. that belonged to Bob Kollar's wife, Eve. Pat, Luci, and her agents drove to the airport and boarded a commercial flight, to the total frustration of the world's society press, which never discovered the honeymoon hideaway.

Presidents' children actually find out what life is going to be like when their father is the country's Chief Executive even before they move into the White House. As soon as a new president is elected in November, his family starts receiving protection even though they won't move in to the executive mansion for another two and a half months.

In November 1968, when Richard Nixon was elected, his daughter Julie was attending Smith College in Northampton, Massachusetts. Right after the election I was assigned to the detail sent to Smith to protect Julie. Those of us on the detail didn't live on campus, but we spent most of our time there.

We maintained a post outside her dorm room throughout the night, and at first our presence was very inhibiting to the other girls on the floor, especially since they shared a communal bathroom at the end of the hallway. When we first arrived, all the girls would scurry past clutching their robes over their nightclothes trying to maintain their composure. As the weeks passed, however, the girls adjusted to our eternal presence on the floor and began to behave normally around us. Everyone became casual again and propriety was discarded, as were most of the robes.

I began to wonder if the girls even noticed us at all anymore. Early one morning, after having been on duty all night, I decided to test just how much we had become fixtures of the floor. I had a newspaper with me, which I folded so a page full of large pictures faced out. Then I turned the paper upside down so that anyone who even glanced at it would notice. Pretty soon I heard a door open as one of the young women came out of her room to go to the bath. I didn't even glance up but sat there engrossed in "reading" my newspaper. As the girl walked by, she slowed her pace. I knew she had seen the paper, but I didn't budge and she continued on down the hallway. As she reached the corner, I saw her looking over her shoulder so I raised my head and gave her a big wink. After a second she broke into laughter, relieved, I think, to find out it had been a joke. That was how I found out the girls did notice us as they walked past.

Anytime Julie was going to leave the dorm, we waited for her in the "dating parlor." I was sitting there one evening waiting for her when one of the other girls in the dorm came over and struck up a conversation. By this time, all the young women on campus knew us and more or less considered us to be part of their lives. Pretty soon a couple of other girls came over and we began joking and sharing the latest campus gossip. Before long, more and more girls joined the impromptu gathering. By the time Julie arrived, she found me sitting in a big armchair in the corner surrounded by a harem of twenty-five or so of her dormmates. Julie seemed surprised, but I just shrugged my shoulders to indicate that I had no idea how it had happened. I said good-bye to the girls and made no explanation to Julie.

Since Julie and the other girls on campus were required to eat all their meals in the college dining hall, Julie's agents also ate there most of the time. The students worked out a system for passing us around during meals. All of the tables seated eight people. Every time we entered the dining room with Julie, there would be two empty seats, each at a different table for the two agents on duty. We were never seated at Julie's table, and we were never seated together. We rotated from table to table at each meal. We never figured out just how the system worked, but it helped to make my assignment at Smith one of the more pleasant ones of my career.

Secret Service agents aren't the stone-faced zombies most of the public perceives them to be from seeing them only on duty around the President. It is true that people watching the President on television or seeing him at a speech or rally will rarely see agents smile, but there is a good reason for that. They are engaged in deadly serious work. Often, however, agents develop genuine and sometimes long-lasting friendships with the people they protect. Still, all agents know they must maintain a discreet distance in public from the people they guard, especially if the protectee is a young, attractive woman or the teenage daughter of the President.

I found out how quickly and easily an innocent remark could be misinterpreted while on a brief assignment with President Ford's daughter, Susan. One summer while she was in high school—before her father became President—Susan worked in the White House book store selling books to visitors for the White House Historical Society. I was friends with the woman who managed the store. One day Susan heard the two of us joking about going out for a drink after work and asked, "What about me?"

I smiled, waved my finger at her, and said in my best "dirty old man" voice, "I'll take care of you later." She laughed and went back to work, and I didn't think about the exchange again until three years later.

Susan, eighteen or nineteen by then and the President's daughter, was chosen queen of the annual Apple Blossom Festival in Winchester, Virginia. I was temporarily assigned to Susan's detail for the festivities. At a reception one evening, in the midst of several people including some prominent Virginia politicians, Susan began kidding me about "trying to put the make on her" when she had just worked at the White House instead of living there.

She was obviously just being friendly and meant no harm, but I quickly whispered to her, "Susan, for goodness' sake, shut up before you get me into trouble."

She understood immediately, but before I warned her, she hadn't thought about the possibility that her joke could get not only me, but also her, into a lot of trouble.

Most of the news media representatives who cover the White House and the First Family on a daily basis understand the Secret Service's role in the lives of the President and his family and would make nothing of a remark like Susan's. But there are reporters working for certain tabloids who would need no more than a line like that to come up with a front-page headline reading something like MARRIED SECRET SERVICE AGENT TRIES TO SEDUCE PRESIDENT'S DAUGHTER. Most agents would rather not have to go in and explain something like that to their supervisors so, whenever possible, they avoid making remarks that could be misconstrued.

Agents sometimes find that their duty to maintain security at the White House entails protecting the privacy of the First Family. It is often difficult to draw the line between the two. Early in President Nixon's first term, Mrs. Nixon arranged a press tour of the First Family's private living quarters on the second floor of the White House. This area is almost always off limits to the press and public and even to most White House staff members unless the President or First Lady invites them there. In other words, this is the one place in the world outside their permanent home where the First Family cannot be disturbed.

There are two sets of reporters who cover the White House—those who cover political issues and those who concern themselves with social events. Because the First Lady's office is in the East Wing of the executive mansion, the latter are called East

Wing reporters. They are frequently even more aggressive than their counterparts who cover political activities in the West Wing. It was for the East Wing "newsies" that Mrs. Nixon conducted a tour of the family's private quarters.

I escorted the dozen or so reporters, all of them women, up to the second floor at the appointed hour. They had been there only a few minutes when I realized that I had made a blunder, not a major breach of security, but something I should have thought of nevertheless. All of the telephones on the floor had the First Family's private numbers listed beneath the buttons for any reporter to see. A photograph of me with a sheepish look on my face, holding a piece of paper over the telephone and surrounded by reporters, later appeared in Winzola McLendon and Scottie Smith's book, *Don't Quote Me.*

Actually, I could have saved myself the trouble of trying to conceal the numbers since at least one of the journalists had already memorized them or copied them down. When she later tried to call the First Lady without going through the White House switchboard and East Wing press office, we had the family's private numbers changed.

The pressure of life in the public eye is especially tough on young children. The only one who lived in the White House during my years in the Secret Service was President Carter's daughter, Amy.

When the Carters moved into the White House in January 1977, Amy was enrolled in a District of Columbia public school. Carter's decision was probably a political one intended to show his support for public education, but where Amy went to school made little difference to the Secret Service. No matter where she went, a detail had to accompany her.

I wasn't on the White House detail during any of the Carter administration, but I was assigned to the Washington field office. Because of my previous experience, I was sometimes assigned to replace White House agents who were sick, on leave, or doing advance work for upcoming presidential trips. Sometimes the assignment was to accompany Amy to school.

Sitting through elementary school classes isn't the most exciting way to spend a day, but it's part of the job if the President's daughter happens to be in fourth grade. Like most agents, I simply took these assignments in stride, figuring that something a little more interesting was bound to come along in a few days.

Normally, agents don't offer any advice to adult members of the President's family unless it pertains directly to security or a family member asks for an opinion on a particular subject. With children, however, it is sometimes a little more difficult to stand back looking official and ignore what is going on around you.

One bitterly cold day I had taken Amy to school and was sitting in the classroom with her. When it was time for recess, the teacher told the children it was too cold for them to play outside. Amy didn't like the idea of staying inside in the least and began throwing the kind of tantrum that is not at all unusual for a ten-year-old who can't do what she wants.

She would be plenty warm if she put on her coat, Amy argued, and her teacher wasn't being fair to her. I wasn't about to override the teacher's decision and take Amy outside while all the other children stayed in the classroom. I listened to her for a while and then called her over, away from her classmates.

"Amy," I said, "I know you have a warm coat and it would be okay for you to go out in it. But not all the children in the class have coats as warm as yours and the teachers have to look out for the best interests of all the students."

She walked away from me still sulking, but she said no more about going out or being treated unfairly.

There are times, however, when Secret Service agents encounter situations that call for action rather then ethics. Like, what do you do when a three-ton elephant attacks the President's daughter?

Amy was attending a pet show at Hickory Hill, Ethel Kennedy's home in McLean, Virginia, just outside Washington. It was a charity fundraiser, and Mrs. Kennedy had arranged to have a circus elephant named Susie for the children to ride. For some reason, Susie decided she didn't like the party and went on a rampage. The crowd scattered and Susie headed straight for Amy, who was about a hundred feet away. Agent John Desmedt grabbed Amy and ran toward a rail fence with her. He handed Amy to an agent across the fence while another member of the detail, Kent Wood, tried to attract Susie's attention. The elephant paid no attention to Wood, however, and the rail fence didn't faze her. She ran right through it.

At a dead run, carrying Amy, with Susie still bearing down on them, the agents reached Mrs. Kennedy's back porch and took their charge inside. The elephant's trainers got her under control shortly and the party continued, but Amy's agents kept a wary eye on Susie.

There are also times when Secret Service agents see adult members of the First Family at less than their shining best. This was the case once when David Eisenhower, President Nixon's son-in-law, was staying at the Nixon compound in Key Biscayne, Florida.

David is a nice guy and he was well liked by most of the agents on the White House detail after he and Julie Nixon married. He was not, however, an especially athletic type. Perhaps because it was his famous grandfather's favorite sport, golf was David's game also. I never saw him play, but I understand he is a pretty good golfer, as was President Eisenhower.

Early one morning, David invited several of the President's weekend guests at Key Biscayne to watch him demonstrate the proper way to hit a tee shot. After a short lecture, he put down a ball, faced the ocean, and drew back his club. When he swung, instead of hitting the ball the way he had just described, the golf club flew out of his hands and sailed straight into the Atlantic.

There wasn't too much anyone could say, so the guests who had witnessed the demonstration just turned and walked back to the house. The agents posted nearby had a difficult time keeping that stern security look on their faces though.

CHAPTER 11

On the Road

I could see the landing lights on Air Force One as the big blue-and-white jet was on the final approach to the airport in Salzburg, Austria. Hundreds of antiwar protesters assembled on the other side of the airport runway saw the plane too. Suddenly, about five hundred of them climbed a fence and marched onto the runway.

A 707 jetliner touches down at more than a hundred miles an hour, and while I doubt any of the protesters had suicide on their minds, it was clear a lot of people were going to be killed unless something was done in a hurry.

I grabbed a radio from a White House advance man and called Bob Taylor, head of the Secret Service detail abroad Air Force One with President Nixon.

"We have demonstrators on the runway," I shouted, "demonstrators on the runway!"

Bob told me to stand by while he notified the pilots. A few seconds later he advised me the President's plane was going into a holding pattern and asked me to keep him informed.

Nixon was stopping in Salzburg on his way to Moscow for his first presidential visit to the Soviet Union. His three-day, low-key state visit had been designed to allow him time to rest and adjust to European time before his meeting with Soviet leader Leonid Brezhnev. Because I speak German, I was assigned to advance the stop. I arrived there nearly a month ahead of the President to make all the security arrangements for the visit. My counterpart in Salzburg was a courtly gentleman just below Cabinet rank in the government—the Austrian equivalent of J. Edgar Hoover. I soon discovered both that nothing could be done without his consent and that he didn't seem to have the slightest idea of how to deal with large demonstrations.

Soon after arriving, I discovered through my own sources that protesters against the Vietnam War were planning to converge on Salzburg from all over Europe to try to disrupt Nixon's visit. When I attempted to discuss this with the Austrian security forces, however, their only response was "Don't worry, we'll take care of it." Despite their reassurances, they never told me how they planned to counter the demonstrations and protect the President and their own top officials.

When I finally pieced together a general picture of their plans, I realized they would be grossly inadequate, but I lacked the authority to change them. The Austrians had never faced the massive demonstrations to which we had become accustomed in the United States. I continually made diplomatic suggestions about crowd control measures and ways to make sure that the militant antiwar leaders of the demonstrators didn't get close to President Nixon and the Austrian Chancellor. Most of my suggestions were ignored.

This worried me particularly because when the President travels overseas, the Secret Service is almost totally dependent on the security forces of the host country to ensure his safety. A team of Secret Service agents surrounds the President when he is on foreign soil, but it is up to the host country to provide the intelligence checks and other protective measures that the service handles when he travels in the United States.

It was apparent that the Austrians were overlooking many small but vitally important details. For instance, they had over two hunderd undercover agents coming into Salzburg from all over the country to help with security but had failed to devise a way for them to recognize each other or to be recognized by the U.S. agents traveling with Nixon. I could just imagine two agents getting into a gun battle because each thought the other was an assassin.

My offer to the Austrian officials to provide lapel pins for their undercover agents, such as we use in the United States, was refused. Austria is a small country, I was told, and the agents would have no trouble identifying each other. I didn't believe it, but, again, there was nothing I could do about it.

As the day of the President's visit drew near, I had two major concerns. First was the demonstrators. It took no more "intelligence" than listening to the radio to determine that an antiwar rally of massive proportions was being planned to coincide with Nixon's arrival. Second was the Austrians' plan to allow spectators on the roof of the airport terminal to watch the arrival ceremony. One look at the building was all it took for anyone to tell it was a perfect position for a sniper. They hadn't even arranged to check the handbags of the people who would be on the roof. The Austrians said people would find it insulting to be searched, and they even refused to set up checkpoints to clear those allowed on the roof. I finally convinced them to permit me to place some U.S. agents up there. At the very least, I felt we should have some friendly guys with guns nearby.

My success in setting up any effective way of dealing with the demonstrators was even more limited. Each time the Austrians showed me their plans, I could detect major flaws.

"How are you going to stop the protesters from reaching the airport?" I kept asking.

Each time the answer was "Don't worry, they will never get to the airport."

On the day of the arrival, my worst fears were realized.

The protesters simply went around the roadblocks the police had established along their announced line of march. By the time Air Force One made its final approach, the situation had gotten totally out of hand.

As soon as I advised Taylor to keep the plane in the air, I went straight to the head of Austrian security, who was waiting along with other dignitaries to greet Nixon. By this time, everyone could see that Air Force One was pulling out of its approach and regaining altitude.

"When you get those people off the runway," I told the Austrian security chief, "I'll bring the President of the United States into this airport."

He said he knew we had an alternate landing site and seemed to believe we had never intended to bring Nixon into Salzburg. I was astonished to hear this. Of course, for a number of reasons—including weather—there is always an alternate landing site for Air Force One, but there had never even been a hint of any plan to bring Nixon into any airport except the one where we were standing and where the President's plane was at that moment trying to land.

"The President is waiting to land right here," I told the Austrian security man. "But he won't until those people are gone and you and I have personally inspected the runway to be sure it's safe."

Even if we could get the demonstrators off the runway, I wasn't about to let Air Force One land without making sure no one had left a bomb out there. And if I was going to get blown up, the guy who was responsible for the mess we were in was damn well going to be with me.

Meanwhile, the Austrian chief of protocol, who was in charge of all the ceremonial functions that were supposed to be taking place, was yelling at the security chief, "Do what he says, do what he says!"

At this point, I was making decisions for the United States government that could have had long-term and potentially serious foreign-relations implications, but I was the guy on the spot and had no other choice.

After a few minutes, a State Department Foreign Service officer who was the number two man in the U.S. Embassy in Austria stepped in and took over the "negotiations." Following a considerable amount of shouting among the Austrian officials, Army troops were ordered to clear the runway. Several hundred Austrian soldiers charged the protesters, using their rifle butts to force them off the runway. They made no attempt to be gentle. I don't know how many of the demonstrators were injured, but when the Austrian security chief and I drove the length of the runway, there were clothes and shoes scattered everywhere. None of these items would prevent Air Force One from making a safe landing, however, so I radioed Bob Taylor to bring the plane in.

Nixon landed twenty minutes late, and we had very few security problems during the remainder of his visit. Perhaps the Austrians decided the U.S. Secret Service knew what it was talking about. In any case, they began following our advice. By the time the President left for Moscow, every Austrian security man was wearing one of the lapel pins I had offered them to begin with.

It is ironic, but when the President travels abroad there are always fewer security problems in Communist countries. In democracies such as the United States, Austria, England, and Australia, citizens are free to express their dissatisfaction with a leader through peaceful demonstrations. When the demonstrations get out of hand the way the one in Salzburg did, something has to be done about it. In Communist countries, there are never any demonstrations. The government simply doesn't permit them.

This difference became quite clear to me when I accompanied President Nixon on his historic visit to China in 1972. We had no idea what to expect when we arrived in Peking. I flew in on an advance plane that landed about half an hour before Air Force One. The Chinese government wouldn't allow us to bring in enough agents for the normal three-shift rotation, so we had to divide the detail into two twelve-hour shifts. I was on the 8-P.M.-to-8-A.M. shift. The day shift flew in with Nixon and we relieved it that evening.

In addition to clothes, most of us also took a suitcase full of food with us, since we weren't sure whether we could safely eat the food in Peking. That turned out to be an unnecessary precaution, however. The food in China was excellent and the Chinese even provided us with American-style steaks and eggs. From a security standpoint, we might as well have left our guns in Washington too. There were only about ten agents on each of the two shifts, plus about ten supervisors—far fewer personnel than normally accompany the President on foreign trips.

When we arrived at the Peking airport, Premier Chou En-lai and a few other top Chinese officials were waiting to greet President and Mrs. Nixon, but there was no crowd. Except for a military honor guard, the airport was virtually deserted.

Throughout the trip, every man on the detail had a feeling of vulnerability. We were in the middle of a country of nearly a billion people and the Chinese officials controlled everything. Unlikely as it was, if they had decided to prevent Nixon from leaving, the Secret Service couldn't have done a thing about it. We would only have been able to stop a lone assassin should one have attacked Nixon, but I believe our presence there was reassuring to the President. At least he was surrounded by familiar faces.

Despite these fears, no security problems arose at any time during the visit, and the Chinese couldn't have been more cordial to the agents accompanying Nixon. We were considered part of the official party and members of the off-duty shift were invited to all official functions as guests. I attended both the state dinner given in Nixon's honor and a performance of the Chinese national opera as a guest. We were driven to these functions in a limousine followed by a Chinese security car—whether to protect us, to watch us, or both, we never knew. We were told we could go anywhere we wanted in Peking. According to the Chinese, no areas were off limits, although each time we walked into the hotel lobby a guide would appear to escort us wherever we were going.

The security of Peking seemed light-years away from the situation we often encountered on Presidential visits to democratic nations that place few restrictions on their citizens.

During a trip to several countries in Asia and the Pacific during the fall of 1966, President Johnson made stops in Melbourne, Sydney, and Brisbane, Australia. The crowds were immense in all three cities, and we had to battle both antiwar demonstrators and Johnson admirers who just wanted to get close to him. During a motorcade through Brisbane, the crowds broke through the barricades lining the street and crushed the agents surrounding Johnson against his limousine. Bob Taylor couldn't move and the car crept forward over his foot, breaking several bones. Wooden sawhorses had been set up across the street from the President's hotel. As Johnson arrived and got out of his car, we heard a crunch as the crowd broke through the barriers. Agents and Brisbane police officers locked arms to form a circle around the President and we finally fought our way inside. Then Johnson, who loved crowds like this, turned around and went back outside. We were ready to kill him ourselves at that point. The crush of bodies was so great that my arm got caught between two people and I couldn't pull it out. My watch was stripped from my wrist, and I didn't know it was gone until sometime later in the hotel when I looked to see what time it was.

This type of thing can happen in the United States or almost anywhere else in the world. Generally, the crowds mean no harm, but they can subject the President, those around him, and themselves to real danger.

Sometimes, especially during the busy primary-election seasons, the problems are caused by young, inexperienced political advance people working for presidential candidates. While the Secret Service always provides a team of advance agents who go in ahead of the President when he travels, it's not always possible to do that for the candidates.

When there are a half-dozen or more people running in presidential primaries and they are all over the country making five, six, or seven stops a day, the service doesn't have the manpower to advance every stop. If the candidate's advance man or woman is inexperienced, problems sometimes arise. Crowd control measures may be inadequate or the candidate's room may not be the easiest to secure. But that is simply one of the prices we pay for living in a democracy where anyone is free to run for president, and I wouldn't have it any other way.

Even worse than American presidential campaigns, from a security standpoint, is taking a president or vice-president to the United Kingdom. The British are usually very restrained and orderly but the Secret Service gets nervous every time someone under its protection sets foot on British soil. The reason for its anxiety is the restriction placed by the British government on the carrying of weapons. Most policemen there go about their duties unarmed, and they expect visiting law-enforcement officers to follow their custom. For many years, only the Secret Service shift actually on duty was allowed to be armed during a presidential visit to any British city. While the restrictions have been modified somewhat by the rise of international terrorism—of which the United Kingdom has seen its share—Secret Service officials would still prefer to have much more firepower at their disposal during a presidential visit. For one thing, unlike the protective forces supplied by an American city the President visits, all of the bobbies lining motorcade routes or surrounding hotels where the President is staying are unarmed.

But while it may sometimes be easier to guard a leader in a totalitarian state than in a free society, being in a Communist country can bring on some nerve-racking situations as well.

Romania was one of the last stops on President Nixon's first major overseas trip, in July 1969, which took him around the world in thirteen days. Because this was the first Communist country he had visited since becoming President earlier that year, we were all a little edgy. We also knew that Nixon was exhausted from traveling and from the number of meetings he had held with various heads of state.

I was working the midnight shift at the hotel where the President was staying. At about 1 A.M., the White House signal-board operator called. He told me that Nixon had been talking on the telephone a few minutes earlier and the line was still open, but no one was talking on it now.

This was highly unusual, of course. I couldn't imagine what the problem might be, so I raced from the command post to Nixon's suite, not knowing what to expect.

The agent on duty outside the suite was startled when I came running up. He said everything was quiet and there was no sign of any problem. Since the agent outside the room couldn't leave his post, I told him about the call I had just received and went into the living room of the President's suite. It was dark, but there was a light coming from the bedroom.

I walked quietly to the door of the President's bedroom and looked in. Nixon was propped up on his pillow with the receiver resting on his right shoulder. He had finished a call, but had fallen asleep before he could hang up. I walked over to the bed, trying to decide whether to remove the phone and risk waking him or just to leave him as he was.

Very slowly, I reached down for the receiver. When my hand was about six inches from his throat, the President woke up with a startled expression on his face.

"The phone was off the hook, Mr. President," I said. "We were concerned that something might be wrong."

Nixon recognized me and relaxed. When I asked if he wanted me to hang up for him, he nodded and was asleep again before I was out of the room. I took the receiver, told the operator everything was fine, hung up, and quietly left the room.

Although I was working that night, I was actually in worse shape physically than the President. The trip had been exhausting for everyone, but I had spent the previous three or four days completely incapacitated, with my fellow agents doing my job for me most of the time. One of our previous stops had been in India. Before any overseas trip, the advance agent sends a report back to Washington noting whether it is safe to eat the food and drink the water in the hotel where the Secret Service detail will be staying. I had read his report before leaving, and it said that there would be no problem with the food at the hotel in New Delhi.

During the trip, however, the hotel where the detail was to stay had been changed, and I had somehow missed that report. I was on the midnight shift when we arrived, so after checking in, I went to the hotel restaurant to have dinner. I should probably have known there might be a problem because I was the only American in the restaurant. I didn't heed this sign, however, and ordered a salad and fish. When my meal arrived, I took a bite of the fish, but it tasted funny. After having a bite or two of the salad and vegetables, I pushed my plate back, paid my check, and left. There was definitely something wrong with the food, but I assumed I hadn't eaten enough of it to bother me.

How wrong I was!

Not long after I went on duty, I became deathly sick. With the severe diarrhea and vomiting I suffered from, there was no way I could stay at my post. An agent from another shift was called to replace me. I made it through the rest of the night before seeing the White House doctor the following morning. He gave me some medicine that probably helped, but I couldn't eat anything for two or three days. I spent most of the time either in bed or in the bathroom as we hopscotched across Asia and through Europe. I was able to work again when we reached Romania, but by the time we arrived back in Washington, I had lost about fifteen pounds. My wife hardly recognized me when I got home, and it took me more than a month to recover fully from three or four bites of food in New Delhi.

The kind of grueling schedule that the White House detail often works can be illustrated by a trip President Johnson made to Hawaii in 1968 for a meeting with South Vietnamese President Nguyen Van Thieu.

This time I was working the 4-P.M.-to-midnight shift. We flew into Hickam Air Force Base near Honolulu on the backup plane. The day shift was aboard Air Force One with the President.

We left Washington in the morning and chased the sun across the Pacific.

Because of the six-hour time difference, we arrived in Hawaii at 2 P.M. local time—two hours before our shift began its watch, but already 8 P.M. "body time."

We just had time to check into a hotel, change clothes, and go to work. We had been up for over sixteen hours and were facing eight hours when our instincts and reflexes were supposed to be at their sharpest.

I have often wondered how effective a Secret Service detail around the President would be if it was faced with an emergency under such circumstances. I know it would rise to the occasion, and once any action started the adrenaline would keep each member going as long as necessary, but human beings can't be as alert when they are dead tired as when they have had a full night's sleep.

Agents are on duty to *prevent* anything from happening to the President, however, not to react after something happens. Standing alone on a post at midnight, not having been to bed for almost twenty-four hours, agents can find it difficult to keep their eyes open, let alone anticipate a threat to security. Such schedules are the price agents pay for being on the Secret Service's "first team" and also the reason why the White House detail is a young man's job.

Those midnight watches in faraway places can bring some of the most rewarding times to agents, though, and produce some of the fondest memories. One of my most vivid recollections of President Nixon comes from just such a night.

I had worked the midnight shift at Camp David one night in December 1972. After being relieved, I drove back home and had time to lie down for about an hour before reporting to Andrews Air Force Base to fly with Nixon to the Azores in the North Atlantic for a meeting with French President Georges Pompidou. Because we flew east on this trip, it was about 10 P.M. when Air Force One landed at Lajes Air Force Base in the Azores, which meant it was almost time for me to go back to work.

My post that night happened to be on the back porch of the house where the President was staying. It was a beautiful night and what seemed like millions of stars were suspended so low over the island you felt you could reach out and touch them.

Inside the house, I could hear that the President had a radio tuned to a National Football League playoff game between the Washington Redskins and the Los Angeles Rams. The Redskins were on their way to the Super Bowl, and Nixon was one of their biggest fans. Throughout the season, he had called Coach George Allen to suggest plays for the team. I doubt that Coach Allen used any of Nixon's plays in the game that night, but Washington won.

After the game ended, the President came out on the porch and began discussing it with me. I am also a Redskins fan and, like Nixon, had followed the season closely. For a half hour we discussed the playoffs, the season, and the Skins' chances in the Super Bowl, just like two guys getting together over a couple of beers to discuss the game, except there was no beer.

That was one of the rare times I got a chance to talk to the

President on a personal basis, and it served another purpose as well. Our conversation helped to keep me awake.

Foreign trips aren't always all work and no play for Secret Service agents, however, as I once discovered in Egypt. I had left the White House detail by this time and been transferred to the Secret Service field office in New Orleans, but because of my experience as an advance agent for foreign trips, I had been called back to the White House temporarily to advance the Egyptian trip. When I arrived in Washington to join the advance team, my agent friends gave me a hard time about accepting an assignment where there would be little chance of meeting any ladies to help pass the off-duty hours.

My years on the White House detail had earned me the nickname the Silver Fox for two reasons—my prematurely gray hair and my reputation, sometimes deserved, sometimes not, as a ladies' man. Although I was married at the time, I enjoyed the company of beautiful women and never made any secret of the fact with my co-workers. Neither did I ever lie about my marital status to the women I met.

My section of the Egyptian advance team went to Alexandria, where Nixon and Egyptian President Anwar Sadat would travel after their initial meetings in Cairo. We stayed at a beautiful old hotel surrounded by lavish gardens and with its own private Mediterranean beach, casino, and disco. There were few guests in the hotel because most tourists had not yet returned to Egypt following the October 1973 Middle East war. I was mentally preparing myself for a couple of weeks of hard work with little off-duty excitement when I went to lunch in the hotel restaurant with several other agents on our first day there. As we sat down at a table, we noticed two attractive women sitting about four tables away.

One of them was strikingly beautiful, with long, flowing dark hair that reached to the middle of her back, and dark brown eyes set off by a deep suntan. After a few minutes at the table, there was eye contact between the two of us, but I saw no way I could simply walk over and strike up a conversation with her. For one thing, I had no idea what language she spoke.

After lunch, I stopped by the hotel desk and asked the clerk where the other people staying in the hotel were from. He told me they were a tour group from Vienna, Austria. My old Irish luck was holding out, I thought. When I'd been stationed in Germany while in the Army, I had made an effort to learn to speak German, and had practiced it every chance I got since that time. So I knew that if I could find a way to meet the beautiful lady in the dining room, at least I could talk to her.

Later that day, I made a point of returning to the hotel to see if I could find her. When I walked out onto the balcony overlooking the beach, there she was. She did wonders for a bikini.

Quickly I went to my room, changed into a bathing suit and went to the beach for a quick swim. I walked along the sand until I reached the area where she was sunning herself. In English, I asked her if she would watch my towel while I went for a swim. In broken English she answered that she was Austrian and didn't speak much English. I immediately switched to German, feeling very proud of myself.

My swim lasted about thirty seconds, because I had to get back to work. But before I left the beach, I learned that her name was Susanne and she agreed to go to dinner with me that evening. We hit it off beautifully, having a long casual dinner and then going to the casino for some gambling and to the disco, where we danced until late in the evening.

When I walked her back to her room, I asked if I could come in to use her phone to call another member of the advance team and find out if there had been any developments during the evening. After my call, she offered me a drink and we went out onto the balcony to talk and listen to the waves roll in from the sea. No one could have asked for a more romantic setting. There was a gentle breeze bringing the aroma of the gardens to the balcony, with the sky full of stars and a full moon reflected in the smooth waters of the Mediterranean. Very soon, I knew that I wouldn't be returning to my own room that evening.

Susanne and I spent the next ten days together. After Nixon and Sadat met in Alexandria, the advance team was sent to Cairo for the final portion of the trip. We took the same train that the two presidents had ridden the previous day when more than a million people had lined the route in a massive show of support for Sadat. Susanne left her tour group and returned to Cairo with me. It was almost as if she had become part of the advance team. All of the other agents had met her and liked her, although I'm sure some of them were a little jealous of me.

The Nile Hilton in Cairo had been reserved for the presidential party, and I was booked into a room with another agent. Susanne and I went to a small hotel nearby to get our own room, but when we tried to check in, the clerk wouldn't allow us to share a room because we weren't married. That was the first time I had seen Susanne's Austrian temper—I thought she was going to drag the clerk across the desk and tear him to pieces. She ripped into him verbally, but it did no good. He said it was Egyptian law and we couldn't share a room. But he did relent enough to give us adjoining rooms, so we ended up with a suite and spent two more nights together in Cairo, dancing the evenings away at an outdoor disco on the banks of the Nile.

The day I was to return to the United States, I called the agent who was making the plane reservations and asked him to book me on the last flight out of Cairo. He called back shortly and said I was on a 6 P.M. plane to Rome, but would have to spend the night there and take a TWA flight to Washington the following morning. When Susanne heard this, she left her tour group altogether and flew to Rome with me, where we spent one more night together. She took me to the airport the next day, and there were a lot of tears at the gate. It was difficult for me to get on the plane for Washington because I would be returning to what, by then, had become a very unhappy marriage, and I was afraid I would never see Susanne again.

My fears were unjustified, however. A few months after I returned from Egypt, my wife Shelby and I agreed that the strain on our marriage was more than either of us needed. While it was difficult to leave my two sons, I knew my marriage had reached the point where I had no other choice. To what degree my problems at home were brought on by the pressures of my job, I can't say, but I know all the midnight shifts and foreign trips and weekend work contributed to them. I believe Shelby understood this to some degree also.

As for Susanne, I would see her again in Paris less than a year after we met in Egypt, and over the next two years we met several more times in cities all over Europe when I got assignments there. I ended the relationship with her after meeting and falling in love with Helenmae, my second wife, and I didn't talk to Susanne again until the summer of 1981.

After H.M. and I separated following the Reagan assassination attempt, I began thinking about Susanne and wondering what had happened to her. It had been over five years since I had heard from her, so I figured she was probably married and possibly had children. But I decided to write a one-page letter to her old address in Vienna. I told her I was single again and wondered what had happened to her. If she was married, I said, I wished her all the best for a good life, but if she wasn't married or involved with anyone, I would like to hear from her. A week later, I got a telegram: DENNY, I AM NOT MARRIED, AND I DO NOT HAVE ANY CHILDREN.

That started a summer of letters and transatlantic telephone calls that ended with Susanne coming to Washington in September for a two-week visit. I feared that she might have changed in five years, but when I saw her walking down the ramp at National Airport, I knew she hadn't changed a bit. She was as beautiful as ever. We spent two wonderful weeks together and have stayed in touch ever since.

In contrast to the trips involving beautiful women and moonlit Mediterranean nights are the times when senior American government officials travel to war zones and unstable Third World countries where, as far as the Secret Service is concerned, everyone is armed and potentially dangerous.

I once accompanied Vice-President Hubert Humphrey to South Vietnam. After meetings with the U.S. military commanders and senior State Department officials in Saigon, Humphrey's schedule called for him to fly to the huge U.S. Marine base at Da Nang to visit wounded troops in the hospital there. The Army and Marines had done all they could to ensure the Vice-President's safety, but Da Nang was still in a combat zone. I flew in to Da Nang a day ahead of Humphrey to advance the hospital stop on a light plane that was hit by small-arms fire, but the pilot managed to land it safely. Shortly after I got to the hospital where Humphrey would present medals to wounded men, the Viet Cong began shelling the base. It was a hair-raising two days, but before the Vice-President arrived, the Marines stationed heavy patrols all around the base and managed to prevent any incoming fire while he was there. As he walked through the wards, pinning medals on pajama-clad Marines, Humphrey was his usual cheerful self, seemingly unconcerned with the danger and living up to his political nickname, the Happy Warrior. But the rest of us kept listening for the telltale whistle of incoming rounds.

At least in Vietnam we had nearly half a million American troops to help protect the Vice-President. Later I also went with Humphrey to Indonesia, where we were the first Americans to arrive after the overthrow of a Communist government. Shortly after we got there, I received a firsthand lesson in the politics of the Third World: the head of security with whom I was working proudly told me that he had killed a next-door neighbor whom he had suspected of being a Communist. After a few days, I became convinced that he would have had no qualms about killing anyone who got in his way. He quizzed me constantly about American security procedures and was particularly interested in "methods for extracting information" from prisoners. I tried to explain things like the First Amendment and "due process of law," but I don't think I convinced him that American security forces don't torture people to get information. He asked me to send him some Secret Service manuals on interrogation and other subjects, which I later did in the hope they might teach him something about democracy. I doubt he got the message, if he read them at all.

During this trip, the Indonesian head of security held a reception for the Secret Service agents who were with Humphrey. There was a band playing and several very pretty young women had been invited for our entertainment. I danced with one of the girls a couple of times, but then she told me she had to go home. I thanked her for the dances and she left. I found out the next day that my host had sent some of his goons after her to bring her back, because he assumed I wanted to go to bed with her and that was what she was there for! Apparently they couldn't find her. To try to get her out of whatever trouble she was in, I made a point of telling the head of security that I really hadn't been interested in her.

Situations like that can be hair raising on foreign trips, but agents needn't be in an exotic land to find themselves in uncomfortable positions. It can happen right here at home, as a friend of mine named Pete Lowell found out during the 1976 presidential campaign.

Pete was assigned to protect Eunice Shriver, whose husband was a Democratic candidate. Mrs. Shriver, a sister of the late president Kennedy's, took her children to the Kennedy family home in Hyannis Port, Massachusetts, during the campaign. Late one evening, she suggested that everyone, including the children, go for a boat ride on the bay. Pete was talking to an attorney on board when he suddenly realized that all of the adults were sitting together in the stern of the boat.

Concerned because it was a dark night and the boat was traveling very fast, Pete asked Mrs. Shriver who was at the helm.

"Oh," she said, "Anthony is driving the boat. He always drives."

The only problem was that Anthony was only six years old and could hardly see over the windshield. Mrs. Shriver believed in giving her children responsibility at an early age, but Pete decided he would go forward and give Anthony a hand with the boat, just in case.

CHAPTER 12

Medal of Valor

The life of a Secret Service agent is filled with extremes. In my case, being an agent for twenty years took me from stakeouts of underworld counterfeiting operations in the slums of New Orleans to a ceremony at the Treasury Department where I received the service's highest award—the Medal of Valor.

The public most often sees the Secret Service performing its mission of protecting the President and other top officials of the government. The majority of the almost two thousand agents employed by the service spend most of their time protecting U.S. currency against counterfeiting, however. Just as the increase in international terrorism has made guarding public officials all the more important, technological advances in the printing industry have made the job of guarding against counterfeiting more important than ever, and more difficult. Because of the precautions taken with the kind of paper and ink used, no one but the Treasury Department's Bureau of Engraving and Printing can produce a perfect twenty- or fifty- or one-hundred-dollar bill. With the printing equipment available today, however, almost any experienced printer can turn out money that would fool just about anyone except an expert.

Fortunately, most printers are honest businessmen who will have nothing to do with illegal schemes. Moreover, most companies that sell printing equipment and supplies cooperate with the Secret Service by reporting any sales that appear to be connected with counterfeiting. But there will always be those who try to make a fast buck, literally.

In 1982, for example, the Secret Service seized over seventy-three million dollars' worth of bogus currency in more than eighty raids on counterfeiting operations. The Treasury Department estimates that in 1982 counterfeiters succeeded in putting into circulation an additional eight million dollars that was not confiscated.

In recent years, most countries have taken more stringent measures against counterfeiting than the United States has. Many have begun using additional colored inks and distinctive watermarks on their bills. Some use special inks that make a portion of the bill appear three-dimensional when viewed from a certain angle.

Numerous studies have determined that the United States should take similar steps. The technology is readily available. A technicolor dollar with a seal printed on its face in silver 3-D ink would certainly make life more difficult for counterfeiters and easier for the Secret Service. For political reasons, however, the government has declined to take such steps. The familiar United States greenback is such an important, familiar, and stable world currency that any radical change in its appearance could be disruptive to the entire international monetary system. So instead of using advanced printing techniques to thwart counterfeiters the government continues to rely on the men and women in more than sixty Secret Service field offices.

Most of my career in the Secret Service dealt with personal protection, but I spent two years in the New Orleans field office during the 1970s. Two counterfeiting cases we dealt with while I was there are typical of the kind of work that goes on most of the time in field offices across the country.

One of these cases involved a large-scale operation that was spread over much of Louisiana and Texas. An informant in Houston told the Secret Service office the name of the man who ran it and that it was centered in New Orleans. The culprit, whose first name was Louie, had been acquitted of a federal counterfeiting charge earlier and had gone around New Orleans bragging about how he had beaten the Secret Service. This time, we were determined to get him. Based on the information from the informant in Texas, we began a full investigation.

The break in the case came when Louie sent one of his girl-friends to Houston with a trunk full of twenty-dollar bills. She passed one in a bar one night, but it wasn't noticed until the next day. The next night, she went back to the same bar and gave the same bartender another fake twenty. He remembered her from the evening before, checked the bill carefully, and called the Secret Service. She was arrested before she left the bar. When agents searched her car, they found several thousand dollars' worth of counterfeit twenties. Confronted with an almost certain prison sentence and the loss of custody of her children, she agreed to become an informant under the Federal Witness Protection Program. We wanted Louie, not her.

Within a few weeks, we had evidence that Louie was counter-feiting not only money, but credit cards and Texas driver's licenses as well. We turned over all of the evidence concerning violations of state law to the Texas Rangers and Louisiana State Police, just in case Louie somehow beat the federal charges again. But this time it wasn't necessary. We seized all of his printing equipment and Louie received a five-year federal prison sentence. We gave his girlfriend a new identity and moved her to another state.

The other case involved a small-time hood who was passing

around bogus money in New Orleans. He wasn't printing the bills, he was just being paid to get rid of counterfeit money that was coming in from New York and New Jersey. Several people were working with him and the money was showing up all over town.

It is virtually impossible to get a conviction against anyone for passing one counterfeit note. All the person has to do in court is claim he or she didn't know the money was counterfeit and has no idea where it came from. To get a conviction, the service must catch someone in possession of a substantial quantity of counterfeit bills or the plates on which they were printed.

An agent does have recourse, however, to perfectly legal ways to make life unpleasant for someone who is known to be involved in counterfeiting. One of the people helping the man we were trying to catch was a woman who worked for a large shipping company in New Orleans. I had solid evidence that she had passed one fake bill in a store. I didn't want to arrest her, but I did want to talk to her. When I called she asked me not to come to her office because she was afraid she might lose her job. I told her to be in my office at ten o'clock the next morning. She said she would be there, but she didn't show up, so I got a warrant for her arrest. With another agent, I went to a restaurant near her office and saw her there eating lunch. I decided to give her the benefit of the doubt. We returned to the office and waited to see if she would call, but she didn't.

Just before it was time for her to leave work, we walked into her office with the warrant. In full view of her co-workers, we read her rights to her, handcuffed her, and led her out of the office. When we returned to the Secret Service office, I took my time filling out the arrest papers. By the time I finished, I knew that the federal magistrate would have gone home for the day and she would be unable to make bond.

She spent the night in jail. By the next morning she was ready to cooperate, but what information she had was of very little use to us.

Later we picked up the steady girlfriend of the man we were trying to catch after he had sent her out to pass some of the phony bills. In the course of our questioning her, she learned that he was seeing several other women and also using them to help distribute the money. After she was released, she went to his house and shot him to death. She was convicted of first degree murder and is serving a life sentence in Louisiana.

Many people think of counterfeiting as a relatively mild white-collar crime in which no one actually gets hurt. While it has sometimes been portrayed this way in books and movies, it doesn't take too long in a Secret Service field office to discover that most counterfeiters are also involved in other criminal activities, frequently drugs and prostitution and sometimes even blackmail and murder.

The two years I spent in New Orleans were the low point of my career. Many Secret Service agents like criminal investigative work and do all they can to avoid protective detail assignments. I was just the opposite. In this regard, the Secret Service is almost like two federal agencies in one. The jobs of protecting the nation's currency and protecting its political leaders are quite disparate. All agents have to be capable of doing both, yet everyone in the service has a preference for one or the other.

I didn't get along very well with the agent in charge of the New Orleans office. Because I had come off the White House detail, he seemed to have the idea that I had been sent by Secret Service headquarters to spy on him. Nothing could have been further from the truth, since I hardly knew anyone at headquarters and certainly had no pull there. Nevertheless, he once tried to burn me for an honest—but admittedly not very smart—mistake.

I got a call to investigate possible counterfeit bills that had turned up in a bar in the section of New Orleans known as Fat City. When I arrived, the owner showed me two fifty-dollar bills received in the bar the night before. They were both counterfeit. I signed a receipt for them and initialed and dated both bills.

Before leaving the bar, I put the two bills into a folder with some paperwork. As I was getting into my car I laid the folder on the roof to get my keys out of my pocket. Then I got into the car and drove away, leaving the folder on top. I had driven only a block or two when I realized what I had done. When I got back to the bar, the folder and papers were still lying in the street but the two fifties were gone. I reported what I had done when I got back to the office, and in a few days the two bills with my initials on them showed up again.

The agent in charge of the New Orleans office reported the incident to Secret Service headquarters with a recommendation that I be reprimanded. The other agents in the office were astonished that he would make such a recommendation. The reply that came back from headquarters said the mistake had obviously been honest and unintentional, and told the New Orleans chief to forget the whole thing. I suppose that convinced him more than ever that I was a spy from headquarters.

After two years in New Orleans, I was glad to get back to Washington and the kind of work I enjoyed. Because of my previous experience in the Intelligence Division and on the White House detail, I spent a good part of the next six years—during which I was assigned to the Washington field office—doing what I liked best: advancing presidential and vice-presidential trips and protecting senior government officials like Secretary of State Kissinger. As a senior agent, I could fill virtually any protection assignment, from taking Amy Carter to school, to filling in for a shift leader at the White House.

The last time I visited the Oval Office as a Secret Service agent, I wasn't on duty. I was there as the President's guest.

In July 1981 President Reagan invited Jerry Parr, Ray Shaddick, Tim McCarthy, and me to the White House to thank us for what we had done that day outside the Washington Hilton. By this time, the President had fully recovered from the wound he'd received in the attempt on his life, and Tim was also well and back on duty. The President spent much of the twenty-minute meeting talking to me about what had happened after I subdued and arrested Hinckley. He was most interested in Hinckley's reactions after he had fired the shots, and wanted to know what Hinckley was like, what he had said to me, and what had happened after the shooting. I had been so intensely involved in the case it hadn't occurred to me that the President knew very little about what had taken place after he had been shot. He had probably read some of the accounts of the shooting, but I was the only person he had talked to who was able to give him a firsthand account of the man who had tried to kill him.

On September 23, 1981, Parr, Shaddick, Tim McCarthy, and I were awarded the Secret Service Medal of Valor, the Treasury Department Exceptional Service Award, and ten thousand dollars each from the federal Special Act Award program.

Secretary of the Treasury Donald T. Regan presented the awards in a ceremony held in the historic Cash Room at the Treasury.

About a hundred guests were invited to the ceremony, but it was very low key. I was extremely proud of the awards I received, but I was also a little bit embarrassed about the recognition I was getting for what I considered part of my job. I'm sure Jerry, Ray, and Tim felt the same way.

The Medal of Valor is the Secret Service's highest award. It has been given only fourteen times in the history of the service. The citation that accompanied the medal reads:

For courageous action in protecting the life of President Ronald W. Reagan on March 30, 1981.
As the President walked to a waiting limousine, shots were fired from a crowd of onlookers. With no regard for his personal safety, Special Agent McCarthy instantly hurled himself on the assailant while he was still firing and assisted in disarming and subduing him.

Special Agent McCarthy's demonstrated willingness to sacrifice his own life in the line of duty was in
the highest tradition of the United States Secret Service.

The Exceptional Service Award is the Treasury Department's
highest commendation and "is conferred by the Secretary on employees who distinguish themselves by exceptional service within
or beyond their required duties."

The Special Act Award, through which we received the ten-
thousand-dollar payment, was established by Congress to "recognize and reward federal employees who perform special acts
in the public interest in connection with their official employ-
ment."

I had to smile when I looked at the check that Secretary Regan
handed to me at the ceremony, however. It was a reminder that I
was, after all, still an employee of the Treasury Department. Instead of being made out for $10,000, the check was for $7,500.
The other $2,500 had been deducted for federal income taxes. I
actually ended up paying some additional tax on the award in
1982 since it put me in a higher bracket.

Three other Secret Service agents also received Special Act
Awards during the ceremony. Agent Russell Miller was com-
mended for moving immediately to take Tim McCarthy's place
on the presidential detail when he saw that Tim was wounded.
Drew Unrue received an award for driving the President from
the Washington Hilton to George Washington University Hospital, part of the way with no police escort, in just three minutes.
Each received a two-thousand-dollar award. And Danny Spriggs,
my partner on the protective intelligence team on March 30, received a one-thousand-dollar Special Act Award for "his aggressive reaction to the assailant while in the direct line of fire, as well
as his restraint in not firing into a crowded area at the assailant."

The week after the awards ceremony in Washington, Parr,

Shaddick, Tim McCarthy, and I were named Policemen of the Year for 1981 by *Parade* magazine in conjunction with the International Association of Chiefs of Police. We attended the police chiefs' annual convention in New Orleans, where we were presented with the Police Service Award for that year.

Parade and the International Association of Chiefs of Police also awarded Officer Thomas K. Delahanty of the Washington police, who had been wounded by one of Hinckley's shots, one of ten honorable mentions in the 1981 Policeman of the Year awards.

Officer Delahanty was forced to take medical retirement from the police department as a result of the wounds he received that day.

Tim McCarthy returned to the White House detail after a three-month recovery from his gunshot wound, but was later transferred back to Chicago, his hometown, where he became the assistant to the agent in charge of the Chicago field office.

When Ray Shaddick's tour of duty on the White House detail ended, he was named agent in charge of the service's Hawaii field office.

Jerry Parr moved from his job as agent in charge of the presidential detail to assistant director of the Secret Service for protective research. That job put him in charge of all the technical aspects of security, including the service's Intelligence Division and its Technical Security Division. He retired from the service in February 1985.

From the summer after the shooting until I retired at the end of 1984, I was the Secret Service liaison officer to the State Department. For those three years, my partner, Agent Lee Privett, and I were responsible for coordinating all interagency functions concerning the Secret Service and the State Department.

After retiring from the service, I formed a private security consulting firm in Washington to advise executives and corporations of ways to prevent assaults and kidnappings.

In looking back over my twenty-year career as a Secret Service agent, I sifted through memories from over half the countries of the world and from every state. There are few occupations that offer the opportunity to see that much of the world.

The attempt on President Reagan's life gave me an opportunity that few men get off the field of battle: I was able to prove to myself that I had the courage to risk my life to do what had to be done. More important to me than the medal and awards I received is the knowledge that I acted with honor.

I will never forget my first assignment to a presidential detail. It was a cold January day in 1965, and I was a rookie agent in the Omaha field office. I had been sent to Washington to augment security for President Johnson's inaugural parade. Along with the memory of my pride, I can still summon up the weight of the responsibility that accompanied it.

There are many other memories, of course, some of which tend to blur together after all these years. I can visualize incidents along motorcade routes, in hotel ballrooms, at airports, but I have no idea what city, or even what country, I was in at the time.

Standing in dark hallways in the middle of the night with nothing to look at hour after hour but blank walls is just as much a part of the fabric of my recollections as the excitement tinged with fear that I felt while fighting off crowds of presidential supporters and adversaries alike.

I have gone from interviews with poor, uneducated check forgers in the slums of New Orleans to meetings with ambassadors and top government officials in a matter of days.

This and more is expected of a Secret Service agent, and I am proud to say I believe I always lived up to the expectations of my colleagues and my country.

If I could choose between pursuing another line of work and doing what I did for twenty years, I have no doubt that I would choose the Secret Service all over again, even though it caused me some sadness and pain along with a lot of happiness.

I feel I have performed a service to the people of the United States and of that, more than of anything else in my life, I will always be proud.

☆

Index